Go Janet!

Mental Training for Runners

JEFF GALLOWAY

MENTAL TRAINING FOR RUNNERS

NO MORE EXCUSES!

Meyer & Meyer Sport

British Library Cataloguing in Publication Data

A catalogue record for this book is available from the British Library

Mental Training for Runners – No More Excuses!

Maidenhead: Meyer & Meyer Sport (UK) Ltd., 2016

ISBN: 978-1-78255-083-9

© 2016 by Meyer & Meyer Sports (UK) Ltd.

Aachen, Auckland, Beirut, Cairo, Cape Town, Dubai, Hägendorf, Hong Kong,

Indianapolis, Manila, New Delhi, Singapore, Sydney, Tehran, Vienna

Member of the World Sport Publishers' Association (WSPA)

Total production by: Print Consult GmbH, Germany, Munich

ISBN 978-1-78255-083-9

E-Mail: info@m-m-sports.com

www.m-m-sports.com

TABLE OF CONTENTS

INTRODUCTION
YOUR INNER STRENGTH—BELIEVE IN IT!

You have within yourself the power to overcome low motivation on the lowest energy days and the power to keep going when there are challenges. By using the proven strategies in this book you can also make permanent nutrition changes, manage stress, and maintain control over fatigue and injury.

You'll also learn how neuroscientists have found that distance running stimulates the growth of new brain cells and improves thinking and learning at any age. Even after a few running steps, brain circuits are turned on for a better attitude, more vitality, and personal empowerment.

We now have proof that running transforms the brain in many positive ways. Revolutionary research begun in the 1990s, made possible by new technology, identified the brain circuits that are turned on when we run. These circuits trigger the release of brain hormones that balance emotions, enhance problem solving, and help us to make better decisions.

With the help of my wife Barbara, who wrote the foreword to this book, I've discovered nuggets of research that explain why some runners stay motivated and some do not, why some perform well and others do not, and why some enjoy their training and others take it like medicine. Leading researchers you will read about in this book are the following:

» Neuroscientist John Ratey, MD, in his breakthrough book *Spark*, explains how exercise activates key circuits and stimulates brain hormones that grow brain cells and improve mental function.
» Scientists Candace Pert, PhD, and Bruce Lipton, PhD, explain the biological and molecular changes that allow us to control our emotions and reformat negative behavior patterns in the subconscious.
» John Sarno, MD, has shown that stress can trigger negative hormones and a pain response—with management techniques.
» Robert Portman, PhD, and John Ivy, PhD, detail the brain circuits involved in eating behaviors with ways of gaining control.

For four decades, I've been researching, trying motivational strategies, tabulating results, and learning from experience. The ideas inside are the latest evolution of a method that has been practiced successfully by thousands. I offer these as one runner to another based upon the success of my clients. As always, seek medical advice for health issues from those who specialize in the area of your issue—especially someone who wants to find a way for you to continue running.

You can do it!

Jeff Galloway

FOREWORD

TO BE HAPPY, JOYOUS, AND CONFIDENT

By Barbara Galloway

When Jeff told me that he was writing a book on motivation, my first thought was, "for what do you want to be motivated?" Most runners have several or several dozen reasons to be and stay motivated. For me, the answer is in the title of this preface. I want to be happy, joyous, and confident.

The late Dr. George Sheehan, cardiologist, philosopher, and *Runner's World* columnist often quoted Emerson who told us to "Be first a good animal." There is a lot of satisfaction when we follow our most natural patterns of exertion—to move, walk, and run. At a fast pace there are more aches, pains, and fatigue. But when you choose a relaxing pace, with the right balance of running and walking, you can be a good, happy, and joyous animal.

I believe Emerson was telling us that we have within ourselves all that we need for happiness. By using our body regularly, which engages our mind and spirit, we improve quality and longevity. Positive things happen when we are first and foremost good, active animals.

For many years, this has been my ultimate motivation. But, like many experiences in life, running begs us to dig deeper. I have made it a mission to search for ideas that can enhance motivation to exercise and to share these with Jeff. The ideas presented in this book have enriched our running experiences, and I hope that you will experience similar benefits.

I'm not going to stop looking and reading. There are so many great ideas, experiences, and opportunities out there.

Get motivated, stay motivated.

Barbara Galloway

PREFACE

TAKING THE PUKING OUT OF RUNNING— MY STORY

At the age of 13, I was a very overweight, lazy kid. I wasn't proud of being fat, and I realized that exercise could be a key to losing my extra baggage. But in my internal priority list, rated above being lean was the avoidance of exercise. I now know that I had programmed myself to believe that it hurt because of some puking incidents after being pushed too hard by a PE coach who wanted to help me get in shape.

Then I enrolled in a school that required male students to engage in strenuous activities or sports after school. Generally, I'm not a fan of forcing kids to exercise, but it worked for me because of the spontaneous fun that emerged from almost every run with the cross-country team. The head coach, Paul Koshewa, was the most lenient in the school and allowed us "options." I initially joined a group of lazy kids who would jog 200 yards to the woods and goof off.

But one day, an older kid who I liked said, "Galloway, you're coming with us today." My anxiety soared because these kids actually ran long distances—3 miles! I had my lazy boy strategy in place: When I reached the protective cover of the woods I would grab my leg, claim I was injured, and throw rocks in the creek as they ran on. But the runners started telling jokes and then gossip about the teachers. I listened at first, huffing and puffing. With a little more fitness I began to participate in the conversations. We shared stories, argued, and more than anything else, enjoyed the fun environment that we created each day.

Within 10 weeks I was hooked on the endorphin experience, and over half a century later, I still am. My grades significantly improved. I discovered that even when things had not been going well at school or personally, the workout with my group turned my attitude around. The bonding resulted in honest friendships based upon mutual respect that have lasted to this day.

But there was something more powerful about the running experience that pulled me out on the roads and trails by myself when the school year ended. The same force was at work years later when my Navy ship pulled into port after three weeks at sea, and I found myself wanting to run before I did anything else. Regardless of how tired or stressed I felt before, I received a boost to mind body and spirit afterward which was life-changing.

After years of study, I came to believe that as the frontal lobe of the brain evolved to give us judgement and perspective, humans have been searching for meaning in life. When we perform certain positive activities, we stimulate brain circuits that trigger biological changes at the cellular level. Brain hormones are also released that change the brain in many positive ways. The bottom line is that after a run we feel good about ourselves and about the quality of our life.

Many are drawn to running because of these powerful and unique rewards. Without the right tools, however, many push too hard, and break something, burn out, even puke like I did. The common and mistaken assumption is that they are not designed to run. I have spent my life finding solutions to problems experienced by hundreds of thousands of runners.

I've discovered that for each challenge there is a cognitive strategy that can allow almost every person to take charge over their plan of action, their mental attitude, and their motivation. A new world opens up for those who have a proven strategy. They become the captains of their ships, navigating challenges, experiencing empowerment, and learning along the way.

So get out there and run!

1 HOW TO STAY MOTIVATED

STRATEGIES THAT ACTIVATE THE BRAIN'S CONTROL CENTER—OVERRIDING THE "MONKEY BRAIN"

Those who have a proven strategy tend to be more successful than those who don't. They also tend to stay motivated, don't give up, work out more often, and enjoy more of their runs. Strategies activate the conscious brain—the executive brain—which allows one to manage attitude as the running experience is managed.

The simple strategies in this book can keep you under the control of the conscious brain as you plan your workouts, focus on mantras, and follow the schedule. You are in the command center, the captain of your ship, maintaining control of your thoughts and actions. You will also find similar strategies for nutrition and staying injury free.

But there is another brain component we often use by default which—under stress—can lower motivation and cause us to lose our focus. This is our ancient subconscious brain, which I will call the *monkey*, or *reflex* brain. This original brain evolved over tens of millions of years and contains thousands of stimulus-response (reflex) behavior patterns.

The reflex brain has a million times the processing capacity compared with the conscious brain. So we rely on it to conduct most of the activities that keep us alive (heart and lung function, blood flow, etc.). In addition, this amazing brain subconsciously interprets hormone signals from various organs and body parts and triggers the release of hormones to correct problems in organ function and to promote healing.

The ancient brain will also take control over habitual activities that we have learned. During the first few times we ride a bicycle, for example, the human brain consciously (and awkwardly at first) drives the body through a series of actions as we fall down and learn to correct mistakes. By repeating the successful behavior patterns regularly, reflex patterns are established, and riding the bicycle becomes more and more automatic. Once a behavior has been learned it is hardwired into the reflex brain, allowing us to pedal down the road subconsciously while the conscious brain solves problems or philosophizes.

But we have another operating system in our mental structure: the conscious brain, in our frontal lobe. This uniquely human brain is a more recent development (only a few million years in the making) and allows us to gain conscious control over a situation. The conscious brain is left free and ready to solve more serious problems, avoid threats, and take action. The circuits that tend to be in the left side of the frontal lobe conduct logical transactions. The right side is the intuitive and creative action center, connecting us to hidden strengths and innovative solutions which are often unexpected.

The natural tendency when we do something that is habitual is to allow the monkey brain to be in charge. For example, once we have learned how to run and have established a routine route with a regular workout pattern, the subconscious brain usually takes over as we start down the road or trail. On many days this is great because the conscious brain can either work out a logical solution in the left side or be entertained and empowered by the right side.

But if we default to the subconscious brain, it will monitor stress—and this can affect motivation. A stress increase greater than normal will stimulate the monkey brain to release anxiety hormones so that you are not so sure about getting out the door, doing the workout you planned, or going the full distance.

As stress increases from heat, cold, precipitation, pace desired, fatigue, goal for the season, or aches and pains, the reflex brain goes into protection mode, and negative attitude hormones are triggered which greatly reduce your motivation to go on and can make you downright miserable. If no conscious action is taken, the monkey brain will reduce blood flow to the digestive system, waste removal system, immune system, and frontal lobe.

The second way that the reflex brain tries to shut you down when under stress is by a condition called tension myositis syndrome (TMS). When the monkey brain becomes overloaded with stress, it subconsciously controls a reduction in blood flow to areas that have been damaged. The resulting pain is much greater than it normally would be for the amount of damage. Many runners have reported to me that their common running injuries have been diagnosed as TMS: plantar fascia, iliotibial band, hamstring, back, knee, neck, etc. When they used the conscious strategies mentioned in this book, the pains went away quite quickly.

You don't have to eliminate or even reduce stress to stop the negative hormones or TMS pain. By using a cognitive strategy, you will shift control to the frontal lobe. The executive brain overrides the monkey brain. Following the mental training programs in this book will help you gain control over your motivation even when under stress and stay positive by stopping the release of negative hormones, while opening up the blood flow to TMS areas. (Main source is John Sarno, MD, *Healing Back Pain*, or *Mindbody Prescription*).

Mental training can also help you access the power of the right brain in the frontal lobe. This can unlock intuitive sources of inner strength, conserve energy, and initiate creative solutions to problems.

Regular mental training will reprogram the reflex brain for any realistic challenge, while also setting up patterns for pushing past barriers, maximizing performance, and even reducing chronic pain. When we are young, we learn many behavior patterns that become embedded into the reflex brain. Some are helpful, and some are counterproductive later in life.

For example, many young runners learn in PE class or in high school sports that they should not walk when they run—that walking is "failure." This is hardwired in many adults who try to take up running and believe that the only way to be a successful runner is to run continuously. Most will reach a certain distance where they hit a fatigue wall or become injured because of this compulsion to run continuously. They feel like failures because they believed in some counterproductive subconscious programming.

But every year, thousands of former non-stop runners reprogram the reflex brain after reading one of my books; attending one of my retreats, schools, or clinics; or joining one of our training groups. The logical reasons for taking strategic walk breaks activate the frontal lobe. Through the reinforcement of the members of a Galloway group or my instruction, they do it. The rewards of endorphins and a positive attitude boost allow them to push through the former wall, recover quickly, and often record faster times. A vibrating timer helps to reinforce the run walk run behavior into a successful pattern, and it becomes hardwired. I hear from dozens of former non-stop runners who used to feel they were a "failure" by taking walk breaks but who now cross the finish line of a marathon, half marathon, 10K, or 5K with the most wonderful feeling of accomplishment experienced in their lives and often with faster times. The reprogramming is complete!

The actions of 1) taking charge over the reflex brain, 2) believing in the method, and 3) performing the mostly gentle training of mind and body will activate the positive attitude circuits and stimulate positive mental hormones.

Note: To access strategies for activating the frontal lobe and leaving the monkey brain behind, skip to the chapter, Mental Training Strategies. The chapter, Your Motivation Training Plan, offers a step-by-step method with tools to stay on a cognitive track and practical tips for specific situations.

2 HOW RUNNING CHANGES YOUR BRAIN (FOR THE BETTER)

Running stimulates the brain in many positive ways. The best resource I've found is *Spark*, written by Dr. John Ratey. He and other neuroscientists have found that exercise turns on your brain in many positive ways.

» Brain circuits are turned on for a better attitude, more vitality, and personal empowerment than any other activity.

» Regular runs stimulate new brain cell growth at any age.

» There is quicker problem-solving after a run.

» Better decisions are made after a run.

» Learning is enhanced after a run.

» Running stimulates hormones that balance emotions.

» The executive brain is turned on for better mental focus.

Energy is the top priority for the human organism. Our human brains developed over several million years to solve problems during the search for food. Starting a run in prehistoric times turned on the circuits to increase the chance of finding food. It is believed that when on a food-gathering mission, the memory circuits were turned on and increased to remember how to find the food, how to find routes to avoid predators, and, most important of all, how to find the way back.

Anthropologists believe that during the period 2 million to 1 million years ago humans were forced to expand their migration range to find food. This was also the period in which our ancestors started moving mostly on two feet (instead of four) and started traveling in groups. All of these challenges greatly expanded their brains.

During the long-distance treks, human traits of trust, cooperation, and mutual care developed.

Running was probably the first form of two-footed locomotion—but was not used often because valuable energy resources were consumed rapidly. Remember that the most common cause of death was starvation, and walking allowed humankind to cover great distance with minimal use of fuel.

But when our ancestors ran, it was usually because of a threat—escaping a predator or jumping over a snake. This stimulated all mind–body systems to work at top capacity.

3 THE MIND–BODY CONNECTION

YOUR MIND–BODY INFORMATION NETWORK SENDS MESSAGES IN SECONDS THAT CONTROL YOUR MOTIVATION

Located in the frontal lobe of your brain is the command center that assigns priorities, allocates resources, and gives direction to cognitive mental activity. Learning, decision-making, and judgement are delegated to the hippocampus area where brain chemicals are stimulated to make important connections and hardwire neurons into successful learned patterns.

At any moment in time, you have a continuous flow of information from billions of cells throughout your body and mind. The signals they send can determine negative or positive reactions in your brain and throughout your body, stimulating the production of attitude-changing hormones that determine how motivated you will feel. By using cognitive strategies to plan your workouts and running regularly, you can exert a great deal of control over what signals are sent—whether the brain hormones are positive or not.

Candace Pert, PhD, in her informative book, *Molecules of Emotion*, explains how the brain is "extremely well connected" to the rest of the body at a molecular level, "so much so that the term mobile brain is an apt description of the psychosomatic network through which intelligent information travels from one system to another."[1]

Secretions of hormones are constantly being produced due to current mental and physical conditions. Pert says that current feelings and beliefs will determine which of these peptide secretions are made. These substances lock onto the receptor molecules on the outer edge of most cells, sending information, giving directions, and significantly affecting our motivation and energy level.

Receptor sites receive information from the outside environment "with information substances such as hormones, antigens, drugs, peptides or neurotransmitters. The information processing occurs at the receptor where the signal to the cell can be modulated by the action of other receptors, the physiology of the cell and even past events and memories of them."[2]

"Peptides (hormones) serve to weave the body's organs and systems into a single web that reacts to both internal and external environmental changes with complex subtly orchestrated responses."[3]

So the old concept that the mind is separate from the body is not correct, according to the research.

---

1   Pert, C. 1997. *Molecules of Emotion*. New York: Scribner, 188.
2   Ibid, 352-353.
3   Ibid, 148.

Here is what molecular biologist Bruce Lipton says about this approach:

"This new perspective on human biology does not view the body as just a mechanical device, but incorporates the role of mind and spirit. This breakthrough in the science of biology is fundamental to healing for it shows us that when we change our perceptions or beliefs we send totally different messages to our cells. In effect, we reprogram them. This new biology reveals why people can have spontaneous remissions or recover from injuries thought to be permanent disabilities."[4]

For more than three decades, I have believed and written that running brings together body, mind, and spirit better than any other activity I have researched or experienced. John Raty, MD, Candace Pert, PhD, Bruce Lipton, PhD, and John Sarno, MD, have analyzed the internal connections throughout our organism and have helped me understand the biological and mental framework which can be used to boost our motivation and tap into our potential.

Here's how Candace Pert explains why we feel so good after "playing" (such as during a good run): "When we are playing, we are stretching our emotional expressive ranges, loosening up our biochemical flow of information, getting unstuck, and healing our feelings"[5]

The mind is a very powerful network of information transmitters embedded throughout the body, connecting most cells. Conscious mental-training techniques can harness this powerful system by sending positive messages. These actions stimulate positive secretions which can change attitude within a few moments.

---

4   Bruce Lipton, PhD, from the foreword to Marie, N. 2004. *Passage of Change*. Phoenix: Inner Eye Publishing
5   Pert, C. 1999. *Molecules of Emotion*, New York: Scribner, 277.

4   STRESS ACTIVATES THE MONKEY BRAIN

STRESS STIMULATES THE REFLEX BRAIN TO TRIGGER A SERIES OF SUBCONSCIOUS ACTIONS THAT RESULT IN LOW MOTIVATION, BURNOUT, PAIN, AND LOSS OF FOCUS

When you allow the monkey brain to be in charge during your run, this reflex brain monitors total stress throughout your mind–body network. When it senses it's "too high," the reflex brain shifts into "protection mode," triggering a series of reactions to reduce motivation—sending negative messages, stimulating secretion of negative mood hormones, and reducing blood flow to damaged areas. Under severe stress the monkey brain will reduce blood flow to the conscious brain, digestive tract, and immune system.

Because blood flow is reduced to the gut, the brain's energy source, blood glucose, is reduced. Lower blood flow and lower fuel supply reduce the conscious brain's ability to take command, allowing the subconscious brain to remain in control.

Stress hormones are subconsciously triggered, and these lock onto receptor molecules. Negative attitude messages are sent and received between the mind and body within a few minutes. If you don't activate the executive brain, the reflex brain will trigger a series of actions to lower motivation and increase doubt and misery.

Pain! Many of your aches and pains may be the result of stress. The overstressed subconscious reflex brain knows the location of current injuries and other damage because it is constantly receiving this information from areas all over the body. As the overall stress load increases (even due to anticipating a hard or tiring workout), the reflex brain will subconsciously reduce blood flow to these areas. This results in pain that would normally not be felt (or would be minimal and manageable without the reduction in blood flow). Dr. John Sarno covers this condition, tension myositis syndrome (TMS) in his books *The Mindbody Prescription*[6] *and Healing Back Pain.* I highly recommend them.

Later in this book you will learn how you can turn your attitude around by taking conscious control, adjusting to realistic goals, setting up several different plans of action, believing in the plans and staying positive. You'll also learn how the mind-body can keep you going while managing stress.

4.1   UNDERSTANDING THE SOURCES OF STRESS AND PRESSURE

Pressure is generated by perceived expectations. We know that our boss, our spouse, our parents, or children each have expectations of various types. Most of this is not communicated, which is too bad. Things get more interesting as we interact with the key people in our lives and encounter conflicting expectations. In many cases, the expectations exceed what we can deliver currently (or ever). *Self-perceived pressure* can produce the greatest stress for most of the runners with whom I've worked. Those who have perfectionist tendencies accumulate the most pressure. In any case, sustained pressure is a major source of stress. But there is hope.

---

6   Sarno, J.E. 1998. *The Mindbody Prescription.* New York: Wellness Central.

SOURCES OF STRESS

Goal stress—Goals can motivate us to run when we might otherwise sleep in and motivate us to push harder when we don't feel like doing so. But on the tough days, we often sense pressure from a looming goal and deadline. Choosing goals that are not realistic is a very common source of pressure—and will make every aspect of the journey more stressful.

Workout stress—Extending the distance of long runs results in greater fatigue at the end. Heat increases this stress. Speed training offers an additional set of challenges. All of these can be managed, but the stress load will increase during the training and trigger low motivation hormones and other protection responses. Good news: In this book you'll find coping strategies for each of these sources.

"Exceeding our speed limit" stress—We usually feel really good at the beginning of the workout, too good. The increased pace or extended distance or reduced run walk run ratio produces a gradual fatigue build-up that is often denied until the muscles are spent. This dramatically increases lingering soreness and muscle weakness for days afterward, which add to the stress load.

Lingering fatigue—When we push past endurance or speed limits by increasing physical workload, most of the fatigue is erased during the rest day after workouts. When the workload is too hard for current ability or not enough rest was allowed, some body parts have pockets of lingering damage. The subconscious brain targets these areas for blood flow restriction when stress is too high (see the TMS section in the glossary).

OTHER SOURCES OF STRESS AND PRESSURE

Primitive genetic programming—These are survival reflexes that were appropriate for hunter-gathers or cavemen, but not for us. An example is anger management issues.

Negative learning—We can learn negative behavior patterns in childhood when we imitated parents, teachers, or coaches who simply did not know the correct methods or concepts (or didn't know they were being imitated). Even when we learn that these early lessons were not logical or right, the childhood programming will trigger anxieties when we embark on a positive method that is in conflict as long as we allow the monkey brain to control our run.

Unresolved issues from childhood or adolescence—These can be very commonly the result of anger and rage during early development from neglect, lack of love and caring, unresolved disputes, no respect, being told that one is a failure, etc.

Current stress from job, family, or other—Most commonly these revolve around continuing life conflict situations that you cannot control. Some examples are the following: You have to work for a boss who makes bad decisions; you and your spouse disagree about some family issue; you want to give your kids some form of freedom, but they are acting suspiciously.

Note: You don't have to eliminate the stress or pressure to get motivated. You need to mentally focus on a realistic plan to shift the control center to the conscious, human brain..

4.2   DIFFUSING STRESS AND PRESSURE

The negative effects of stress and pressure are only a problem if we let the subconscious monkey brain be in charge. To reach our potential for running enjoyment while also maintaining motivation at a high level, we must have a cognitive strategy to deal with the situation. Each positive step you take will empower your conscious brain to take control away from the subconscious.

» You don't have to eliminate the stress to be motivated, but you must acknowledge it. Honesty is the best policy, and denial results in more stress later.

» You must acknowledge that stress is causing the pain and loss of motivation or mental focus. Until you take conscious action to be aware of what is going on, the subconscious brain will control the situation, causing it to become more negative. Just a statement to yourself ("I am under stress and I'm going to deal with it") is the first step that will engage the conscious frontal lobe to take control over subconscious reflex thoughts and actions.

» Consciously acknowledging each source of stress will help you deal with it and stay on track. Remember that you don't have to resolve the issue or eliminate it. Simply say to yourself that you know that these specific stresses are bothering you.

POSITIVE STEPS

1. Develop a coping strategy that allows the conscious left brain to override the sub-conscious reflex brain. Follow the plans in the chapter, Mental Training Strategies. Just telling yourself that you have a plan and believing in the plan can change the secretions of hormones and start the positive emotional messages which are communicated between your mind and body.

2. Pressure can be acknowledged and managed by communicating with the people who have expectations. It is appropriate to ask the question: "What are your expectations of me in this area?" A simple conversation with key people can set up positive plans for understanding, adjusting, and then managing the expectations. Taking action in each area will continue to give you more control over the situation and improve attitude.

3. Through mental training, the subconscious reflex brain can be reprogrammed. In the chapter, Mental Training Strategies, you will learn how to break up the stressful challenges into a series of steps. This makes the task doable, which continues to stimulate the positive secretions, and the peptides transmit positive messages through the mind–body network.

4. Gentle running with the right run walk run ratio will produce endorphins. These create a positive shift by themselves. Endorphins are powerful attitude adjusters.

5. A series of positive actions generate momentum. The mind and body sense that things are improving, which lowers stress. As we move our feet and legs, walking and running toward the workout goal for that day, we turn on brain circuits which secrete brain hormones. Combined with positive mantras and thoughts, you can move your mental attitude into the positive direction you need as you open up the blood flow to key areas.

4.3   TOOLS THAT GIVE YOU CONTROL

Most of the runners I've worked with on motivational issues have brought most of the stress on themselves. In many cases the individual doesn't understand the principles of training or of setting up a realistic goal. In each case listed next, you'll find the leading sources of stress or pressure when running, along with the page in this book where you can find the conscious actions necessary to gain control.

» **The goal is too challenging**—See the "Magic Mile" section on page 124. I ask beginners to run the first race "to finish." After the first one, a realistic improvement can be motivating. But when the goal is not realistic or at the edge of possibility, more stress is generated through doubt, uncertainty, and the tough training needed to prepare for the goal. You can believe in the magic mile as a predictor of your best possible performance as noted in the section listed. Then, you can make adjustments for non-ideal conditions. This puts you in charge, reducing stress while promoting positive peptide production. The result: a better attitude.

» **Not being prepared for the race**—Look at the section on training balance to reduce stress on page 104. Having a long run of 26 miles before a marathon, compared with a long one of 22 miles or less, has dramatically improved motivation during the last month before the race and during the race (according to those who have tried it both ways). As you blend the elements into a team, you gain control over your destiny. This makes your belief stronger and improves positive attitude hormones and motivation.

» **Running too fast on long runs**—See the section on long-run pace on page 126.
   Note: Long run pace should be no faster than 2 min/mi slower than current marathon pace potential. In my experience, the leading cause of injury and burnout among runners has been exceeding the speed limit on long runs or not taking walk breaks frequently enough. Most runners who do this don't know the pace is too fast. Runners who used to experience burnout by going too fast usually improve attitude significantly by slowing down to a pace that they know they can run. There is no benefit in running long runs faster, and I've not found a long-run pace that is too slow.

» **Running too far before taking a walk break**—See the section on run walk run on page 156. By taking walk breaks more frequently, you'll receive a better endorphin effect and reduce physical stress. On some days, the run segments can be adjusted according to how you feel. On long runs, take the most gentle ratio.

» **Low blood sugar**—Read the "Cognitive Focus on Adequate Blood Sugar = Motivation" section on page 160. Low blood sugar is a major source of stress because this is your brain's only fuel source. The reflex brain monitors the level carefully and stimulates negative peptides when low. It's easy to boost the level.

» **Workout stress**—See the section on realistic goals on page 127. If the goal is too challenging for current ability level, the speed work will be too fast, and the results of races will be frustrating. This increases stress load.

» **Injury symptoms and injury stress**—See the section, "Troubleshooting Form-Related Injuries," on page 145. Do your best to determine whether it's an injury or TMS. If it's an injury, you need to take at least three to five days off to start the healing and then reduce the training load to stay below the threshold of irritation. But the pain from your weak links could be TMS (p. 82). This occurs when stress on the reflex brain reduces blood flow to these body parts, causing pain that is much greater than the damage would indicate. By acknowledging that stress is the cause and letting the frontal lobe take charge, you can open the blood flow and keep training. As always, consult your doctor about medical issues.

4.4   THE STRESS OF TOP PERFORMANCE

THE MORE CHALLENGING THE TRAINING, THE GREATER THE STRESS.

Physical training can motivate and bring us to the brink of top performance. But as the stress builds up, the reflex brain goes into protection mode, shutting off blood flow and stimulating negative hormones that lock into the receptor site on molecules in the body and mind. Successful world-class athletes have intuitively developed cognitive methods to keep going under stress. These methods activate the human brain so that the subconscious brain doesn't shift into protection mode. This cognitive focus can turn the attitude around under difficult and stressful conditions. The first step is having a plan to diffuse the stress.

During the first week or two of a new training program, a challenging goal can increase motivation. But as the workouts get harder, fatigue and aches increase, and it gets harder to run longer at the fast pace—the monkey brain will trigger anxiety hormones. Combine this with fatigue stress, and that darned reflex brain will release negative motivation peptides, resulting in a negative emotional mental environment.

But demanding workouts are necessary for top performance. By taking a series of conscious steps, we can 1) analyze whether aches are possible injuries and take action and 2) keep going with positive thoughts when we feel monkey brain anxiety. By cognitively focusing on one step at a time in a tough workout, we train mind and body to do the same thing when we get into our goal race.

But pushing too hard, for the individual, will trigger the release of stress hormones that can lower motivation. Lingering fatigue adds to the stress. When the body is pushed to its limits, the reflex brain initiates a protection mode response (see glossary). This causes a significant reduction of blood flow to the brain, the gut, and the immune system—as blood flow is increased to the limbs. Corticosterone, a steroid hormone that is associated with depression and reduced motivation, is produced to repair damage.

WHAT HAPPENS WHEN WE TRAIN TOO HARD

» Negative hormones triggered by the reflex brain under stress activate negative thoughts.

» Blood flow is constricted to areas of damage, causing pain and a TMS reaction (see glossary).

» Blood flow is reduced to the gut, significantly reducing absorption of fluids and blood sugar (the brain's fuel).

» Normal repair and replacement of cells is suspended.

» Stress stimulates hormone secretions that quickly change emotions to a negative orientation.

» We are not motivated to continue at a level of performance of which we are currently capable.

» Under repeated stressful workouts, competitive runners get sick. The protection mode reduces blood flow to the immune system, opening the door to infections.

  › Opportunity: You can take conscious action in each area using the programs in the chapter, Mental Training Program, page 52.

  › Do a reality check on the goal to make sure it is not too demanding, page 127.

  › Adjust speed sessions, and do the workload while reducing the stress (e.g., rest interval adjustments).

  › Read the section in the glossary on TMS and prepare to deal with it.

  › Some mental training can be paired with workouts.

> ❭ Reduce mechanical stress by using the ankle. See page 138.
> ❭ Do what works for you.

4.5 MANAGING UNRESOLVED ISSUES

When a person has experienced chronic pain or lingering depression, there are often unresolved subconscious stress issues, stimulating the reflex brain to reduce blood flow to areas that are damaged. Dr. Sarno has an in-depth discussion of this in his book, *The Mindbody Prescription.* His insight and advice have been very helpful for those with these issues, and I highly recommend this book.

» The problem does not have to be resolved, but it must be acknowledged.

» Internal rage from childhood issues is a common cause.

» Complex interpersonal issues are included in this category: Issues after a divorce, having to follow orders from a boss that one does not respect, and concern for parents or children that seem unresolvable.

Vent! At the beginning of a run, express your anger or rage. Shout if necessary. Argue with the absent adversary. Get in a good anger release. Then get on with the run. When you are angry or frustrated, the monkey brain will take you on an emotional roller coaster unless you take conscious mental action. Shouting your thoughts or saying statements to yourself activates the executive brain in the frontal lobe which overrides the emotional brain. With the conscious brain in charge, there is less chance that the subconscious will cause problems during the run. The natural calming effect of the run will stimulate mood-altering brain hormones, allowing you to feel better within a few minutes—and often for hours afterward.

TAPPING OR EMOTIONAL FREEDOM TECHNIQUE (EFT)

Barbara Galloway has introduced me to *tapping,* which can also help you shift from a cycle of monkey brain emotions under stress to cognitive control, step by step. Visit the website of the founder, Gary Craig, at www.emofree.com, or do a search for "Gold Standard EFT Therapy". Another source is Nick Ortner's book, *The Tapping Solution*. For diet issues, search "Jessica Ortner, Weight Control."

5 MENTAL TRAINING STRATEGIES

TAKING CONTROL BY PROGRAMMING YOURSELF FOR SUCCESS

When I told her I was writing a book on motivation, my wife Barbara asked "for what do you want to be motivated?" At first, most runners tend to answer with specifics: to finish a long run in the upright position, to run faster at a given distance, to finish ahead of a sister, neighbor, age group competitor, to qualify for Boston, or, my favorite, to enjoy every run. The specific goal helps the runner maintain cognitive focus at the beginning of a goal-oriented program.

But as you have discovered in the earlier sections of this book, the major challenge in maintaining motivation is maintaining focus as the workouts become more routine and the stress increases. A successful mental training program will reduce stress to a manageable level so that almost every run can bring joy and personal empowerment. The stage is then set for planning a realistic approach to your goal.

Have a goal for each run. This cognitive mental action can activate the executive brain as the warm-up switches on the good attitude circuit. As you think about each aspect of the workout, you can keep the human brain in charge. Without such focus, mental action will often drift under the control of the monkey brain which turns negative under stress and releases hormones that stimulate negative messages, such as "I'm too busy to run," "I'll get too tired," "It's not my day," and "Why am I doing this?"

In the previous chapter, several strategies are offered for diffusing stress. In each case you will be taking conscious action, shifting control away from the subconscious reflex brain. Dr. Lipton explains the power of the conscious components of the frontal lobe:

"Endowed with the ability to be self-reflective, the self-conscious mind is extremely powerful. It can observe any programmed behavior we are engaged in, evaluate the behavior and consciously decide to change the program. We can actively choose how to respond to most environmental signals and whether we even want to respond at all. The conscious mind's capacity to override the subconscious mind's preprogrammed behaviors in the foundation of free will ."[7]

So by acknowledging the stress, maintaining mental focus, and using mantras when needed, you'll produce positive peptides each step of the workout. The next step is to set up an ongoing mental training program that will "run you through" the anticipated challenges each day through a series of doable steps. This will desensitize you to the negative messages, while also giving you a plan with thoughts and words that will help you stay in the frontal lobe during that workout. As you refine and repeat the plan, you reprogram the brain to continue under adversity. This improves your sense of belief in the system, which will stimulate positive attitude circuits and hormones.

The following three mental training methods have helped tens of thousands to overcome motivational issues and be successful. In each case you are training the conscious brain to take control under a variety of challenges. You can do the mental training during a run, while driving, during a quiet time in the morning or evening, or whenever works for you.

---

7   Bruce Lipton, PhD, from the foreword to Marie, N. 2004. *Passage of Change*. Phoenix: Inner Eye Publishing

Early morning mental training can get you focused for that day. Going through the plan in the evening can consolidate issues from the day and prepare for action the next day. When you combine the physical and mental training, you change the brain to take action quickly and efficiently.

Each of these mental methods will turn on the conscious brain and empower the creative and intuitive right side. For top performance you will need to keep activating this executive brain. The mental training can mold them into a balanced team as you stay on track to the goal for that day.

Even with a plan, workout or race stress will continue to stimulate negative attitude peptide production. So it is natural to flip control several times during a hard workout or race. Your conscious action to insert an extra walk break, repeat a mantra, and desensitize yourself to negative messages will help you maintain control over emotions by reactivating the human brain.

Maintaining control over stress is important throughout each workout and during the training program journey. Most of the workout stress can be controlled by using the tools in the section on diffusing running stress in the previous chapter. Continue to explore ways of dealing with your individual issues.

When the stress is too high, frontal lobe activity can be reduced or shut off temporarily. Adjusting to a slightly more conservative run walk run strategy will help to keep stress in balance better than any single adjustment I have found. For example, if you have been running for 2 minutes and walking for 30 seconds, try a few rotations of 60 seconds run/30 seconds walk (or better, 30/30) to catch up.

Desensitizing—You will get to know the adversities of performance or endurance during the long runs and speed workouts. Write down the doubts and negative messages that you have received. Rehearse these and write down a response to each one. This maintains cognitive control. For example:

When you get the message, "This is not your day," talk back by saying, "I can do it!"

When you hear, "You're losing strength," say, "I feel strong!"

Aches and pains—See the TMS section in the glossary and the first chapter.

It is important to know when you have really damaged something or are just under the influence of TMS. Don't hesitate to consult a doctor who wants you to continue running. He or she can help to draw the line.

Continuous increase in fatigue is a reality on long workouts. You can run with significant fatigue as long as you are within the guidelines of pacing and run walk run ratios. Don't push on when there is pain—walk for one to three minutes. On long runs you will get the same endurance even if you walk the last half.

Low blood sugar level (BSL) will increase stress, negative peptides, resulting in reduced mental focus. Candace Pert, PhD, notes that blood glucose supports the ability of the neurons to store and secrete all of the messenger chemicals—neurotransmitters and neuropeptides. So a lower BSL means lower transmissions.[8] Eating a blood sugar booster is a simple fix. See the chapter on this topic in this book.

So let's now move on to the mental training techniques that can desensitize you to the stress build-up and prepare you to keep going at a realistic pace when it's really tough. Whether you are just trying to get out the door to run three days a week or are pushing through strenuous speed training for a Boston Marathon qualifier, the principles are the same.

But you need a plan if you want to maximize your potential. With a plan you'll have more control over attitude, energy level, mental focus, and life itself. The sustaining rewards come from finding out a bit more about who you are, choosing goals that are realistic, and finding that you have more strength inside during challenges than you ever thought possible.

---

8   Pert, C. 1997. *Molecules of Emotion*. New York: Scribner.
     Lipton , B. 2005. *Biology of Belief*. Carlsbad: Hay House, Inc., 103.

6   YOUR MOTIVATION TRAINING PLAN

Yes, you can train your mind to be motivated, just as you train your body to run farther and faster. Just having a plan that you believe in sets up a positive mental environment. Focusing on one small (and doable) step at a time will reduce stress and activate the human brain. By moving from one step to the next, you maintain mental momentum and take control over your motivation and your training. As you do this over and over, you reprogram the monkey brain so that the process becomes easier and easier. Here are the major cognitive actions:

1.   **Do a reality check on your goal.** Make sure that it is within your current capabilities and that you have enough time to perform the key workouts with rest for rebuilding in-between. Keep evaluating your goals and adjust as you head toward the key dates on your calendar. This maintains conscious control over the process.

2. **Acknowledge that the reflex brain responds to stress by secreting negative hormones to lower motivation.** Under severe stress, the subconscious brain will reduce blood flow to gut, frontal lobe, and damaged areas to create pain, lower blood sugar level, and reduce your mental focus. Start talking to the reflex brain when this starts to happen, laugh, and tell it to open up the blood flow. This keeps you under conscious control.

3. **Diffuse the stress by using one or more of the simple methods in this book.** Keep telling that monkey brain that you know what it is doing and that you will not let this happen. This sounds silly, but it's a frontal lobe activation strategy.

4. **Move forward by walking.** Even if you are not going to run immediately, walk around the room thinking through the next steps in the "Jump Start" program below. Use the mantras that help you shift gears. The conscious shift to positive thoughts can change your mood in a few minutes, by turning on the good attitude circuit.

5. **When it is time for your run, go through the following "Jump-Start Your Motivation" program.** Each step keeps you focused. Tell yourself, "I'm in control!"

6. **Identify the challenges you want to manage or overcome.** During the run or other quiet periods (e.g., driving in a car, waiting for a flight or meeting), list the negative messages you receive and the problems in past experiences. Then rehearse yourself through each situation.

7. **Concentrate on one challenge at a time.** Several common ones are presented in the chapter, Situations, with success strategies.

8. **Break up the challenge into a series of small steps that take you from the beginning of the first hints of the challenge to the successful finish.** Only focus on the next step—not the end result.

9. **Mentally rehearse the steps during various quiet periods of your day.** Even if you don't know the solution to problems that come up, rehearse yourself digging down, getting through it, and finishing with a great feeling of accomplishment.

10. **Turn on the brain circuits needed to get the job done and move from one step to the next when confronted with the challenge.** When you repeat the rehearsal and fine-tune it, you are reprogramming the conscious brain to take charge. As long as you have the challenge, continue the regular rehearsal, adjusting to your situation and making it better and better.

A REALITY CHECK ON YOUR GOAL

(Fill in the blanks and do the math so see if you are ready for your goal.)

Goal Distance:

Goal Time:

Magic Mile Time:

Add 33 seconds for 5K pace:

Multiply by 1.15 for 10K pace:

Multiply by 1.2 for half marathon pace:

Multiply by 1.3 for marathon pace:

Add 2 minutes to the marathon pace prediction for long-run pace:

I understand that the pace predictions are based on perfect conditions and my doing all of the training on the time goal program. Agree_____

I understand that on the first race at any distance, a long-run training pace is recommended for the first three-quarters of the distance on race day. Agree_____

Note: Training pace is at least 2 minutes per mile slower than the prediction made by the magic mile.

JUMP-START YOUR MOTIVATION

By activating our human brain when we are running, we can gain control over motivation. But most of the time we let the ancient, subconscious monkey brain govern our running. On short, easy runs, this may not a problem. But as the distance and the pace increase, the exertion and increased body temperature will increase our stress.

If the monkey brain is in control during a stress build-up, it will trigger the release of anxiety and negative attitude hormones, lowering our motivation. You don't have to eliminate the stress to manage and do away with the negative hormones. By taking conscious action, you activate the human brain which overrides the subconscious brain and can bolster motivation within a few minutes.

Each of the following simple cognitive actions can improve mental attitude in every workout as they stimulate the secretion of the positive attitude hormones that make you feel better physically and emotionally. As you take one conscious step after another, you take control of your attitude and your running experience.

» **Eat a blood sugar boosting snack if needed**—Low blood sugar is a major stress on the brain. A simple snack of about 100 calories can often change attitude in 20 to 30 minutes. Some runners have had a rebound by taking a sip or two of a sugar beverage and spitting it out.

» **Drink a cup of coffee**—if you drink coffee and have no problems doing so. Caffeine is a central nervous system stimulant and helps with focus. Even one cup of coffee has been shown to increase the endurance time on a treadmill.

» **Start walking**—The gentle motion of walking will stimulate good secretions of peptides, improving mood and motivation.

» **Smile**—Smiles not only activate positive hormones that lock into molecules and result in good emotions, but they also turn on a brain circuit that bestows confidence.

» **Breathe in cadence with your steps**—Rhythmical breathing has been shown to activate the human brain, reduce stress, and give us a sense of control. Take a lower lung breath every third or fourth breath.

» **Believe that you will feel better and that you are doing something positive for yourself**—Your positive belief in what you are doing activates positive hormones.

» **Lower the adversity of the workout or race**—If you are feeling stress or pressure when considering a pace of 14 min/mi, then run 15 min/mi. If a run walk run strategy of run 60 seconds/walk 30 seconds seems challenging, use 30/30, 20/20, or 15/15. Shorter running segments often leave you feeling so strong that you increase speed at the end—or at least feel strong at the end. (Be sure to get over to the side of the road to take walk breaks and use a beeping timer to signal to fellow runners).

»   **Mantras**—Talk to yourself. You can create your own or use the following:

I'm moving—I feel good.

I know I can do this.

I'm feeling better.

The positive peptides are being received—I feel better.

I'm changing my attitude.

My exertion is making me feel better.

One more minute.

30 more seconds.

10 more seconds.

One more step, one more step, one more step.

7 NO MORE EXCUSES

All of us have days when we don't feel like exercising. Occasionally, you may need a day off due to sickness or too much physical activity. But usually this is not the case. Blame your excuses on the monkey brain which is monitoring stress and wants to reduce the possibility of further increase. Perceived workout stress triggers negative hormones which make us feel unmotivated. Believing in these messages will stimulate negative attitude peptides. Once you quickly decide whether there is a medical reason for these concerns, you'll usually conclude that the reflex brain is just trying to make you lazy.

Thinking ahead and organizing your day will reduce or eliminate most of these excuses. This activates the conscious brain which shifts control away from the reflex brain. You'll find pockets of time, more energy, quality time with kids, and more enjoyment in the exertion. You'll tend to be more productive in everything you do because you have had your time to yourself.

The following is a list of excuses that most of us hear on a regular basis. With each, there's a strategy for blasting them away. Most of the time, it's as simple as just getting out there. Remember, you can be the captain of your ship. If you take charge over your schedule and your attitude, you will shift control away from the reflex brain and turn on the powerful conscious brain circuits while increasing the flow of positive peptides. This leads to improved motivation to exercise. As you set up patterns for dealing with each excuse, it's possible to rewire the reflex brain into patterns that get you out the door.

As you move away from each excuse, turn the words in the positive direction and start moving:

"One foot in front of the other."

"The endorphins are flowing."

"The excuses are melting away."

"Life is good!"

"MY_____ HURTS!"

Most of us have several weak links. These areas of the body are the first to hurt when we are stressed and talk to us more on the days when we have more stress. If there is no inflammation, loss of function, or real pain, it is usually OK to exercise. Indeed, exercise releases the stress which can erase or reduce the pains as endorphins are secreted, killing the pain. But if you have any medical concerns, talk to a doctor who wants you to keep exercising.

It's a physiological fact that stress can greatly aggravate the symptoms of your weak links. Read the TMS sections in the glossary and the chapter, Situations. You'll find more information about this in *The Mindbody Prescription* by Dr. John Sarno. While there is almost always some aggravation in an area of pain, stress can trigger the reflex brain to reduce the blood supply and aggravate the nerve response, producing an increase in the intensity of the symptoms. Gentle exercise can bring blood flow to the area while it releases stress. As you will see in the chapter, Situations, you can reduce or stop this TMS problem by shifting control to the conscious brain.

"I DON'T HAVE TIME TO EXERCISE."

Most of the recent US presidents have been regular exercisers, as well as most of their vice presidents. Are you busier than the president? You don't have to exercise for 30 minutes straight. You will get the same benefit from your weekday workouts by doing them in pockets of time: 5 minutes here, 10 minutes there. Many who start an exercise program find that they don't need as much sleep as they get in better shape, and exercising for 30 minutes or so gets the brain and the body jump-started better than anything else. It all gets down to the question, are you going to take control over the organization of your day or not? Spend a few minutes in the morning to arrange your schedule. By making time for exercise, you'll also tend to be more productive and efficient and will "pay back" the time. Bottom line is that you have the time—seize it, and you will have more quality in your life. Your loved ones will appreciate this, too, because after a workout, you're nicer to them.

TIP: CRAMPED FOR TIME? JUST WALK OR RUN FOR 5 MINUTES.

The main reason that runners don't make progress is that they don't exercise three times a week. Whatever it takes to do this, do it! Even if you only have 5 to 10 minutes, you will maintain most of the adaptations. Besides, if you start with the idea of going out for 5 minutes, you'll usually stay out for 10 or 15 or, often, 30 minutes.

"PEOPLE WILL TALK ABOUT ME."

Many people deprive themselves of the personal empowerment and the attitude boost of running because they are afraid that someone driving by will see them exercising and judge them in some way. Actually, most people admire and respect those who spend the energy to exercise—whether they look like athletes or not. Besides, it's not a good idea to let the opinions of unknown people stop you from doing something that can enhance your life.

"EXERCISE MAKES ME TIRED."

If this happens, you are the one responsible. You have almost complete control over this situation. By starting each walk or run with a good blood sugar level and pacing conservatively with sufficient shuffle or walk breaks, you will feel better and more energized than before you started. If you have a bad habit of going too fast in the beginning, then get control over yourself! As you learn to slow down, you'll go farther and have more energy at the end and afterwards. Be sure to have a snack that's between 100 to 300 calories within 30 minutes of finishing the run. It's best to have 80% of the calories from simple carbohydrate and 20% from protein.

"I DON'T HAVE THE RIGHT BUILD (OR TECHNIQUE) FOR EXERCISE."

Just go to any big marathon and you'll see an amazing diversity of body types—including those who weigh more than 300 pounds. Virtually every one of us is genetically designed to walk or run, and when we do so regularly, our movements become more and more efficient and natural. Even if you don't have smooth form, you can enjoy the way you feel during and afterward. With all of the different pieces of equipment, you can find one that will work for you.

"I NEED TO SPEND SOME TIME WITH MY KIDS."

There are a number of exercise strollers that allow parents to walk or run with their kids. My wife Barbara and I logged thousands of miles with our first child, Brennan, in a single baby jogger. We got a twin carrier after Westin was born. With the right pacing, you can talk to the kids about anything, and they can't run or crawl away.

You can also run-walk around a playground as you watch them play or run around a track while they play on the infield. Home equipment allows busy moms and dads to get in their workout as they watch kids napping or watching TV, or talk with them while they are playing.

"I'VE GOT TOO MUCH WORK TO DO."

There will always be work to do. Several surveys have found that runners are about 30 minutes per day more productive than when they did not run. A good morning run (when paced correctly) can leave you with more energy and a better attitude while you prepare to manage your day. Studies also show that better decisions are made and problem-solving improves after a run. All of this comes with an erasure of stress. Hundreds of morning exercisers have told me that during the quiet morning exercise, they plan their day and solve problems. Others say that the after-work workout relieved stress, tied up some of the mental loose ends from the office, and allowed for a transition to home life. You will get as much (probably more) work done each day if you work out regularly.

"I DON'T HAVE THE ENERGY TO EXERCISE TODAY."

This is one of the easier ones to solve. Most of the exercisers who've consulted me about this excuse had not been eating enough times a day. I don't mean eating more food. In most cases, the quantity of food is reduced. By eating about every two to three hours, most feel energized more often. Even if you aren't eating well during the day, you can overcome low blood sugar by having a booster snack about an hour before a workout. Caffeine, taken about an hour before exercise, helps (as long as you don't have caffeine sensitivities). The dynamic food duo that I use is an energy bar and a cup of coffee. Just carry some convenient food with you at all times. Finally, an easy warm-up run will turn on brain circuits for more vitality the rest of the day.

"I DON'T HAVE MY RUNNING SHOES AND CLOTHES WITH ME."

Load up an old bag or backpack with a pair of running shoes, a top for both winter and summer, socks, shorts and warm-up pants, towel, deodorant, baby wipes, and anything else you would need for exercise and clean-up. Put the bag next to the front door or in the trunk of your car. Then, the next time you are waiting to pick up your child, you can do a quick change in the restroom and make some loops around the field, school, or wherever.

PRIMARY CAUSES OF LOW MOTIVATION

» Time goals are the primary reward from running.

» Goals are unrealistic at present.

» Not enough rest between stress workouts.

» Running too hard most running days.

» Not enough "joy runs" each week.

» Not enough walk breaks in long runs and sometimes other runs.

» Running with a group that is too fast for you.

» Feeling sorry for yourself because you have no support.

» No consistent plan.

» The training plan used is too stressful for you.

8 MENTAL TRAINING PROGRAMS

YOU CAN GAIN CONTROL OVER YOUR ATTITUDE, YOUR PERFORMANCE, AND YOUR PAIN

» Training programs can help you shift from the monkey brain to the conscious brain.
» Take charge over motivation and improve attitude—with positive mantras and easy running.
» Use rehearsal drills—break up a task into doable parts performed step by step.
» Magic words tap into successful patterns and our intuitive and creative powers.
» Dirty tricks will distract your reflex brain and activate the frontal lobe.
» You can learn how to manage and eliminate pain's hold over your motivation.

The choice is yours. You can take control over your attitude, or you can let your monkey brain go through a series of negative reactions that usually result in low motivation and reduced performance. By using the proven strategies in this chapter, you can turn a negative attitude into a positive one, reprogram the reflex brain to stay on track to a positive goal, and tap into the incredible powers of the right brain. Whether you struggle to get out the door when running by yourself or you need more motivation to keep going when it's tough, you have a better chance of success when you have a strategy. This is your motivational training program.

To understand motivation, look inside the mental command and response center—your human, conscious brain. If you don't focus on each aspect of your workout, however, you can allow the subconscious monkey brain to be in charge. When stress accumulates to a significant level, this emotional production center takes protection action to reduce motivation and reduce effort level.

If the subconscious brain is conducting your run (which is common) and stress builds up, a stream of negative attitude hormones are released that trigger feelings that make us want to slow down, quit the workout, or avoid starting the workout. The reflex brain also reduces blood flow to the frontal cortex and to areas of damage that it has already identified. This results in a sensation of pain that normally would not be felt by the damage alone. This pain is the result of TMS.

Note: I am not suggesting that you should run through pain when there is chance of a serious injury. When you have pain in a weak link area that you suspect is an injury, check with your doctor to verify. In many cases, the pain is stress-induced TMS and can be managed cognitively.

By engaging the conscious brain in the frontal lobe, we can usually stay on track and very possibly push to a higher level of performance—even when there is significant stress. See the section on confronting TMS in the chapter, Situations.

The first step is to go through the stress diffusion procedure in the chapter, "Stress Activates the Monkey Brain". Then you are ready to go through a series of mental training drills that will reprogram your reflex brain. With the conscious brain always in charge, you can back off the effort if there is a legitimate health or safety issue (very rare), or check your magic mile to ensure that your goal is not out of your current range of ability.

These drills can allow you to move from one doable step to the next. By managing pace and diffusing stress, the creative and intuitive right side of the human brain can be active and search for solutions to current problems with connections to your inner resources—your spirit.

8.1   MENTAL TRAINING METHOD #1 REHEARSING SUCCESS

Rehearsal has been used for generations by successful individuals in various fields to achieve potential on any given day, even when challenged and under stress. Mentally envisioning a series of steps that deal with the various challenges and rewards activates the human brain to gear up the mind–body team to work together and get the job done.

1.   Rehearsing realistic fatigue, aches and pains, negative messages, and doubts desensitizes us to the challenges.
2.   A series of small steps. The conscious frontal lobe reprograms the reflex brain to stay focused by breaking down a challenge into segments, one leading automatically to the next to the successful finish.
3.   As the rehearsal is repeated and fine-tuned, the conscious brain focuses on one step and then the next to the finish—success.

Rehearsal drills are listed in the chapter, Situations, with step-by-step formats. These are a good start for most runners but need to be adapted to the individual. The principles are as follows.

What—This is a mental storyline of how you want the experience to unfold. At first, you may focus on specific parts of a workout or race that have been challenging for you. You may continue to rehearse only the challenging parts or weave the challenges and solutions into a continuous preview of the whole experience. Most runners "fast forward" through the less challenging segments and focus on the issues that have caused problems. A runner experienced at rehearsal will move though a marathon rehearsal within a matter of two to three minutes at the end of a season.

When—Rehearsals can be done during a run, when driving, in the shower, or waiting for a flight, for example. Trying out the rehearsal during a hard workout can help you fine-tune it to be more effective. Many go through key rehearsal segments during long runs.

Be realistic and positive—The effectiveness of this mental drill will depend upon your being honest about the real challenges, rehearsing through them, making adjustments, and digging down, but always getting though with pride, satisfaction, and a great sense of accomplishment.

Desensitize—Revisit the negative messages that have come up or the physical challenges that could happen during the event. As you visualize feeling these, focus on moving to the next step, but don't think about any of the negatives or surprises that could add stress during the event.

Rehearse the problem, even if you don't know the solution—By envisioning a past problem that you haven't solved, including your digging down and getting through it, you empower the creative and intuitive right conscious brain to find solutions. It often does this by race day.

A series of small steps—Challenges are not confronted head-on, but segmented into doable units. So when there is a significant hill that you are worried about, you visualize shortening the run segments, shortening stride length, accomplishing one segment at a time, and not focusing on the top of the hill until you are congratulating yourself for moving over the top, smoothly gliding down the other side.

Each segment leads automatically to the next—By rehearsing the segments attached to one another, you are more likely to move from one to the next when you get into the challenge.

Rehearse a variety of weather conditions, aches, and pains—As you envision a variety of possible challenges (with actions to deal with them), you will not only be better prepared for what could happen, but you will also train the various body–mind components to work as a team to get the job done.

Finish with a vision of success and accomplishment—Always rehearse success that is realistic. Yes, you feel tired, but you kept going, got through the tough patches, and crossed the finish with strength and dignity.

Note: The actual rehearsal drills are in the chapter, Situations. Be sure to read the testimonials in the chapter, Inspirational Stories.

8.2   MENTAL TRAINING METHOD #2
MAGIC WORDS

Even the most motivated person has periods during a tough workout or race when he or she lets the monkey brain take over under stress and feels like abandoning the goal. By using a successful brainwashing technique, you can use the resources from past successes to pull yourself through these negative thoughts and feel like a champion at the end. By attaching key words or phrases to past successes, you can pull yourself through future challenges.

Think back and identify the problems that you face in your tough workouts or races. These are the ones that are most likely to challenge you again. As you go through a series of speed sessions and long runs, write down the ones that cause you to slow down or want to quit. Go back in your memory bank and pull out instances when you started to lose motivation due to these but finished and overcame the challenge.

Note: This process activates your human brain to recognize the approach of problems, take action sooner to prevent or cope with it, and find resources.

MY THREE MAGIC WORDS: RELAX.......POWER......GLIDE

In really tough runs, I have three challenges that occur over and over:

1. I become tense when I get really tired and worried that I will struggle badly at the end. RELAX is the antidote.
2. I feel the loss of the bounce and strength I had at the beginning and worry that there will be no strength later. POWER is the magic word.
3. My form starts to get ragged, and I worry about further deterioration of running form and muscle capacity due to wobbling. GLIDE has pulled me though.

The problems themselves are almost never serious. The key word is "worry." When you focus on the negative possibilities, you stimulate negative hormones and build anxiety. This adds stress to the reflex brain, which will trigger more negative attitude peptides. So by focusing on problems, you will lose motivation.

My big motivational breakthrough was learning to counter these three problems with the magic words, "Relax...Power....Glide." The visualization of each of these positives shifts mental control to the conscious frontal lobe of the brain. The real magic comes from the association I have made with hundreds of successful experiences when I started to lose it in one of the three areas but overcame the problems. Each time I run through one or more of the challenges, I associate the experience with these magic words and add to the magic. Positive peptides are released, attitude improves, stress is released, and confidence improves.

Now, when one of these situations begins, I repeat the three words over and over. Instead of increasing my anxiety, the repetition of the words calms me down and shifts action to the frontal lobe. Even though I don't feel as strong in the last mile as I did in the first one, I'm empowered just by knowing that I have a strategy and can draw upon my past experience (more positive attitude hormones are secreted). And when my legs lose the efficient path and bounce, the right brain is empowered to take over and make adjustments and find inner strength to go on as it has in past successes.

When I say magic words that are associated with successful experience, there are three positive effects as the conscious brain takes over:

1. The saying of the words shifts you into the human brain which triggers the release of positive memories and the confidence from overcoming the problems before. The monkey brain stops the production of the anxiety and negative hormones.
2. The second effect may be more powerful. The words directly link you to the right brain, which works intuitively to make the same connections that allowed you solve the problems before (e.g., shortening stride, adjusting pace, lower lung breathing).
3. You may get down the road a mile or three before the challenges come on again.

To be successful on any day, you must first finish the race. Most of the time, you can get through the bad parts by not giving up and simply putting one foot in front of the other. As you push beyond the negative monkey brain feelings and the negative hormones go away due to use of the human brain, you create the confidence to do this again and again. Each time you use the magic words and feel the results, it gets easier and more efficient.

Each time you have another success with the magic words, debrief yourself as you ride home:

"What a great run today."

"I started to lose focus and slow down at 5 miles; monkey brain made me feel I couldn't maintain pace."

"I said, RELAX, POWER, GLIDE, probably 15 times."

"With each saying, I felt a bit stronger, and my form felt smoother."

"It took three other episodes of using magic words, and I ran better than I have in years."

"RELAX, POWER, GLIDE worked again on the beautiful Nordic trails at our Tahoe running retreat."

Feel free to use my magic words or develop your own. The more experiences you have associated with the words, the more magic.

8.3 MENTAL TRAINING METHOD #3 PLAYING DIRTY TRICKS ON THE REFLEX BRAIN

The strategy of the rehearsal drill will get you focused and organized, while also reducing the stress for the first third to half of the race or workout. Magic words will pull you along through most of the remaining challenging sessions. But on the really rough days, it helps to have some dirty tricks to play on the reflex brain.

These are quick fixes that distract the monkey brain's emotional hormone secretions for a while, allowing you to keep going for the next segment of the workout or race. These imaginative and sometimes crazy images don't have to have any logic behind them. But when you focus on a creative thought, you activate the conscious brain, which will stop the production of negative messages.

This can change the peptides from negative to positive. Having fun with these visualizations will unlock more positive hormones, improving confidence and attitude.

A shift to creative images can further shift action to the right side of the conscious brain. This often triggers a series of creative thoughts that can entertain you. Once engaged, the right brain can subconsciously solve problems, dig into your inner resolve to keep going, and find hidden strength.

THE GIANT, INVISIBLE RUBBER BAND

When I get tired at the end of a hard race, I unpack this secret weapon and throw it around someone ahead of me—or someone who had the audacity to pass me. For a while, the person doesn't realize that he or she has been looped and continues to push onward while I get the benefit of being pulled along. After a minute or two of mentally projecting myself into this image, I have to laugh for believing in such an absurd notion. When you take charge over the situation by projecting a set of behaviors and acting on them, you activate the conscious brain to take control. Furthermore, laughing activates the creative, resourceful right side of the frontal lobe. This usually generates several more entertaining ideas, especially when you do this on a regular basis.

The right brain has millions of dirty and entertaining tricks. Once you get it rolling, you're likely to receive intuitive solutions to current problems. It can entertain you as you get closer to your finish step by step. Most important, this circuit can empower the legs, feet, and muscles to do what they are capable of doing on that day. The result will often surprise you.

MORE DIRTY TRICKS:

» **The jet engine behind you**
   When you start to slow down, imagine that there is jet engine from a giant 777 aircraft that is blasting you from behind. Run in this tailwind.

» **Oxygen molecules in your shirt**
   When you are feeling the fatigue from a hard run, tap your shirt 3 times and inhale. There are powerful oxygen molecules released that will help to revive your muscles.

» **Bouncy air pads on your feet**
   During the last third of your race when you feel that the feet aren't bouncing any more, turn on the mental switch that inserts air into the skin on the bottom of your feet. It is only activated if you shorten stride and keep your feet low to the ground

9 MANTRAS

SAY THESE AND TURN ON THE EXECUTIVE BRAIN

Athletes have used key words or phrases for generations. These short statements shift control to the frontal lobe, while they activate positive attitude hormones. Keep using them, and you can push back the negative and increase the positive. Try these out during your runs so that you will feel comfortable with them. When needed, you'll be ready.

Have fun with these. Combine several that make you feel strong. Get into a rhythm. Make up a little lyric and sing them.

MANTRAS THAT WORK AT ANY TIME:

Don't give up.

I can do it.

This is my day.

I'm feeling better.

I feel good.

I am strong.

I have control.

I'm getting it done.

I feel confident.

I'm running smooth.

I will prevail.

The spirit is strong.

TALK TO YOUR WORKHORSES:

Heart—Great pumping action.

Heart—Send the blood.

Blood—Bring the oxygen, bring the energy.

Blood—Remove the damage.

Blood capillaries—Open up, good flow.

Feet—Light touch.

Feet—Good turnover.

Feet—Quick and light.

Feet—Low to the ground.

Muscles—Pump the blood.

Legs—Stay strong.

Legs—Smooth motion.

Knees—Not perfect, but working.

Lungs—More oxygen.

Lungs—Working better.

Lungs—Clean the blood.

Body—Everything working together.

Body—Smooth running machine.

Endorphins—Hit me.

Endorphins—I feel good.

Endorphins—Flowing better.

Endorphins—Make me feel so good.

Mind–body—Great teamwork.

Mind–body—Get it done.

Mind–body—A powerful team.

Mind–body—Solving problems.

Tight muscles—Go away lactic acid.

Oxygen—Go to the muscles.

Sugar—Go to the brain.

Blood—Flow, flow, flow.

WHEN IT GETS TOUGH:

One more mile.

One more minute.

One more step.

I have reserve strength.

I can do it.

I feel empowered.

I can push through fatigue.

I am doing it.

The finish is closer.

The strength is there.

THE VISION:

I want to run.

I am a runner.

I am free.

I can feel the accomplishment.

Finish line—I feel it.

The stress is leaving.

The energy is increasing.

The endorphins are flowing.

I'm being pulled to the finish.

I'm pulled along with the flow.

The crowd is pushing.

I'm getting energy from the crowd.

There's energy moving together.

I feel the energy of others.

We're helping one another.

I'm feeling stronger.

I've got mental momentum.

I've pushed through the wall.

I'm going to finish with strength.

I'm improving the quality of my life.

I'm improving.

I am better.

I am fit.

I'm running like Phidippides.

I'm continuing the marathon tradition.

2,500 years of history—I'm part of it.

I'm smiling.

I'm breathing life into my body.

DISTRACTIONS FROM NEGATIVE THOUGHTS:

Where could I move that sign?

How would I redesign that building?

What type of house would I build here?

Where would I live in this neighborhood?

What role would that person play in my novel?

What can I do to help that person get into running?

Where would I put a running trail in this neighborhood?

TALK TO SPECTATORS AND TO VOLUNTEERS:

Thank you for cheering.

Thank you for being here.

You can join us next year.

Thanks for your energy.

Thank you for helping me improve my life.

FUNNY MANTRAS:

I'm running like [a funny character].

I'm dancing.

I'm running on thin ice.

TALKING TO THE PAIN MANTRAS (WALK A BIT MORE ON THE WALK BREAKS AND SMILE):

Brain, I know what you are doing.

Open up blood flow to my [foot, leg, hamstring, etc].

I feel better, now open up more blood.

Blood flow, blood flow.

Endorphins—flow in there.

I need more endorphins—come on in.

10 SITUATIONS

REHEARSING SUCCESS AND PROGRAMMING THE REFLEX BRAIN

Rehearsals develop patterns of thinking and patterns of motion that can shift brain function into the frontal lobe and take cognitive control over your workout or race. If you mentally rehearse these often enough, you will get into a groove to deal with the problems that occur while staying focused on the goal for the day. In a challenging situation, you don't want to have to think about the stress or the challenge. If you have rehearsed a successful plan of action enough times, you can move from one step to the next—almost automatically. Each of these mental rehearsals is a cognitive workout in which the conscious brain sets up a format for a series of actions, edits and refines it based upon the challenges and opportunities, and then goes into action when in the situation itself.

10.1 GETTING OUT THE DOOR EARLY IN THE MORNING

The most common motivational problem, as presented to me by runners over the last three decades, is how to get out of bed early enough and be ready to do a long run, hard workout or race, or simply a run that was assigned for that day—before the temperature rises or before work.

State your desired outcome: To be awake and fully engaged in the run from the start.

Identify the challenge: Monkey brain desire to lie in bed and no desire to exert yourself so early. The stress of the alarm clock and having to think about what to do next when waking up so early.

Break up the challenge into a series of actions, which lead you through the mental barriers, not one of which is stressful.

1. The night before, lay out your running clothes and shoes (often near the coffee machine) so that you don't have to think about it in the morning.
2. Set your alarm, and as you are lying in bed, say to yourself over and over, "ALARM OFF.....FEET ON FLOOR....TO THE KITCHEN." Or, more simply stated, "ALARM....FEET.... KITCHEN."

As you repeat this, you consciously visualize doing each action, connecting them together into a chain of behaviors. By repeating it, you lull yourself to sleep. More important, you have also been programming yourself to take action the next morning.

1. The alarm goes off. You shut it off, put feet on the floor, and head to the kitchen—mentally focusing on each action—because you programmed your conscious brain to take control.
2. You're focusing on each action, putting on one piece of clothing at a time, sipping coffee (or whatever morning drink you have), never thinking about exercise.
3. With coffee cup in hand and clothes on, you stick your head out the door to see what the weather is like.
4. Driving to the workout or race, sipping your beverage, you rehearse seeing friends, feeling the positive energy of an event, easing into the workout or race, and feeling good about your exertion.

5. OR, you walk to the edge of your property, put the coffee cup down, and cross the street. You're on your way.

6. The endorphins are kicking in. The positive peptides are rising. You feel good. You want to continue.

Principle of motivational physics: A body on the bed wants to stay on the bed. But once a body is in motion, it wants to stay in motion.

10.2 GETTING OUT THE DOOR AFTER WORK, SCHOOL, OR A TOUGH DAY

Many runners must run in the afternoon but commonly feel drained at the end of the day. This is another instance of the reflex brain responding to the stress of the day, often due to low blood sugar which triggers negative peptides that leave you feeling tired and unmotivated.

State your desired outcome: To get out the door and start running down the road.

Identify the challenge: Monkey brain has a significant level of stress from the day and if allowed to be in control will sense more stress from a workout, stimulating negative mood hormones that result in a negative attitude about anything but hitting the couch or bed.

Reduce stress as you are driving or walking home by saying, "I'm going to get home, put on some comfortable clothes, and eat and drink." This reduces stress in several ways. There is no thought given to running, and even the thought of eating and drinking can stimulate positive peptides.

1. Put on some comfortable clothes and shoes—that just happen to be running attire.

2. Eat an easily digestible energy snack and drink water or a caffeinated beverage (if OK with you). Caffeine can shift a negative mood very effectively.

3. Think relaxing thoughts.

4. Stick your head out the door to check the weather.

5. Walk around outside to see what's going on.

6. Cross the street, and you're on your way.

Principle of lazy physics: A body on the couch wants to stay on the couch. But once a body is in motion, it wants to stay in motion.

Break up the challenge into a series of actions, and use your conscious brain to lead you step by step through the mental barriers.

10.3   FINISHING A TOUGH WORKOUT

You're into a hard workout, and you are really tired. You're drifting between the conscious desire to get in a good effort and the influence of the monkey brain, which increasingly stimulates negative attitude hormones. As the fatigue rises, the monkey brain triggers messages, such as "This isn't your day," or "You can't reach your goal today," "Just slow down a little," "There are other days to work hard," or "Do this workout again when you are more motivated."

Shift into human brain control by evaluating whether there is a real medical reason why you can't run as projected. If there is a reason, back off and conserve—there will be another day.

Almost every time, however, the problem is very simple: You are not willing to push through the discomfort. *You are letting your reflex brain keep you from your goal.* To do your best in a race, you must learn how to deal with these problems in workouts. As you push through the motivational slumps you will develop the internal resources to do so when you have even more challenges later. By following the steps below you will shift into the human, conscious brain which will override the negative actions of the monkey brain.

Focus on the next segment of the workout. If you have one mile left, tell your conscious brain that you are going to run a quarter of a mile. As you start to run at an okay pace and focus on a distance you know you can finish, you produce positive hormones, and your attitude shift begins. Passing one quarter mile you consciously agree to do another quarter of a mile and then congratulate yourself for moving forward. Segment by segment you get through the mile and feel good about completing the mile. More positive secretions push your mood upward and keep the negative emotions away.

Say positive things: "I'm pushing back my barriers." "I'm overcoming challenges." "This is making me tougher." As you add to the number of repetitions each workout and talk to the frontal lobe, you lock into a series of steps to get through the fatigue at the end of the workout. By the time you run the goal race, the frontal lobe is ready to take action, one positive step at a time.

Confront monkey negative brain emotions with strength statements: Don't quit! I can do it! Mental toughness starts with simply not giving up. Just ignore the negative messages, stay focused on the next few steps, and talk to yourself. This keeps control in the frontal lobe and away from the reflex brain. Positive affirmations activate positive peptides.

10.4   I CAN DO THE NEXT SEGMENT

Champions feel the same discomfort—they just consciously hang on longer and get through it.

In your tough workouts, practice the following drill. Fine-tune this so that when you run your goal race or experience another tough day, you will have a strategy for staying under the control of the conscious brain—mentally tough, triggering a stream of positive peptides.

The scene: You're getting very tired. You'd really like to call it quits, or at least slow down significantly.

Quick strategies: Break up the remaining workout into segments that you know you can do.
» 1 more minute: Run for one minute, and then reduce pace slightly for a few seconds. Then say, "One more minute" and pick up the pace again. Do this again and again.
» 10 more steps: Run about 10 steps, take a couple of easy steps, and then say, "Ten more steps" while picking up the pace again.
» 1 more step: Keep saying this over and over—you'll get there.

Take some gliding breaks:
» Reduce the tension on your leg muscles and feet by gliding for a few strides every 30 seconds. The acceleration-glider drill prepares you for this moment, particularly when coasting downhill.
» As you say, "I'm gliding" or "I'm running smoothly," you continue the mental shift to the conscious brain and focus on positive statements.

Segment by segment:

» If you really question your ability to get through the workout, start each repetition or race segment by saying to yourself, "Just one more" (even if you have four to go) or "Ten more steps—I'm getting it done!"

» Teamwork! If you are on a team or have made a communication pact with a friend, you can pull motivation from the others. Think about your team members and say to yourself, "I feel your strength." The perception of team bonding can pull you through many difficult workouts as you take conscious control and stimulate positive attitude hormones.

» When you are getting close to the end and really feel like you can't keep going, say, "I am tough," "I can endure," "Yes I can," or "One more step."

» Smile!

10.5   FINISHING A TOUGH RACE

At any stage of a hard race, even in the first third, you can encounter problems that add stress, stimulate monkey brain negative hormones, and make you feel progressively less motivated. If you focus on positive, cognitive mantras, you can turn your brain around.

» Desensitize yourself in your mental race rehearsal by listing every negative stress feeling you have had in hard workouts and races. It often helps to say to yourself, "I'm going to feel like slowing down; I'm going to want to give up; I'm going to lose my motivation."

» Confront each negative with a positive statement:

The negative is...	The positive is...
"Back off, this isn't my day."	"Don't give up!"
"There are other races."	"I can do it today!"
"Why am I doing this?"	"I'm empowering myself!"

» Evaluate whether there is a real medical reason (which is rare). If there is a health problem, back off and conserve—there will be another day.

Most commonly, the monkey brain is responding to the stress build-up of the race by triggering negative peptides, creating a negative emotional environment. A successful strategy during the first onset of this attitude downturn is to glide a little. If needed, take a short walk break (15-20 seconds) to mentally regroup and focus on the next segment of the race.

» Activate your rhythmic breathing (mentioned in the in the section, "Jump-Start Your Motivation," on page 42. Smile and start running again with a light touch and smooth cadence. Each one of these actions engages the frontal lobe and stimulates the positive peptides to transmit a message of hope throughout the body.

» To do your best in a race, you must manage the stress build-up by using a routine such as the following. You are training yourself to keep going, which is 90% of the battle. You are also programming the conscious brain to regularly check on the reflex brain, stop the negative thoughts, and insert positive beliefs.

Note: None of these drills are cast in stone. Adapt them to your needs and strengths. You will continue to adapt them as you move through the process.

» Continue to confront monkey brain emotions with strength statements: **Don't quit! I can do it!**
In your speed workouts, practice the following drill. Fine-tune this so that when you run your goal race, you will have a strategy for staying mentally focused and positive. Your belief in a plan will activate brain circuits which can get the job done.

The scene: You're getting very tired and stressed in a race. You'd really like to call it quits, or at least slow down significantly.

Quick strategies:
» Break up the remaining race into segments that you know you can do.
» 1 more minute: Run for one minute, and then reduce pace slightly for a few seconds. Then say, "One more minute" again and again. (You can even use 30 or 15 seconds.)
» 10 more steps: Run about 10 steps, take a couple of easy steps, and then say, "Ten more steps."
» 1 more step: Keep saying this over and over—you'll get there.
» Take an extra walk break to gather yourself, if you need it.

» Take some gliding breaks. By doing the acceleration-glider drill, you will be prepared to do this in the race. You can actually insert three to four acceleration-glider or cadence drills when you feel you are slowing down.

» Reduce the tension on your leg muscles and feet by gliding for a few strides every one to two minutes. The acceleration-glider drill prepares you for this moment, particularly when coasting downhill.

Segment by segment:

» In the race, if you really question your ability to finish, start each mile by saying to yourself, "Just one more" (even if you have four to go), "One more minute," or "Ten more steps." You'll make it the whole way.

» Teamwork! If you are on a team, your teammates need you to finish, and you need your teammates to finish. The commitment to a friend or larger group can pull you through many difficult workouts or races. Even having a long-distance friend who you are going to report to helps to pull you through a tough run. Some runners bring their cellphones on long runs and call their friends as lifelines.

» When you are getting close to the end and really feel like you can't keep going, say to yourself, "I am tough; I can endure; yes I can; one more step."

I CAN DO IT....I AM DOING IT....I DID IT!

10.6 COMING BACK FROM AN INJURY

If there has been orthopedic damage that has kept you from running, make sure that the area has healed enough to start walking. Get clearance from a doctor who wants you to get back into running as soon as you can. When given permission, start with a 10-minute walk and always walk or run with a relatively short stride, feet low to the ground. Every other day, extend the walk by three to five minutes until you reach 30 minutes. Then, insert a 5- to 10-second jog every minute into your walk. If this is too much for you at first, walk the second half of the workout—or do what you can do. After a day in which you have inserted the running segments into your walk, take the next day off from running. You can walk on the rest day if you are not having problems from walking.

Note: This constant interaction and adjustment of run walk run keeps you focused and in control of your executive brain.

Your goal is to finish each run-walk feeling like you could continue for another 10 minutes or more without any huffing and puffing. When you feel comfortable at 5- to 10-second run/60-second walk for 30 minutes, extend the time by 5 minutes one day a week (usually the weekend), every other weekend, until you reach an hour. On the shorter weekend, stay at 30 to 40 minutes. Shift to doing two other runs a week (usually Tuesday and Thursday) and increase the amount of running. When 10/50 feels too easy on the shorter runs, move up to 10/40. After three to six of these workouts, shift to 10/30. You could either stay at one of those strategies or continue to gradually increase to 15-30, then 15/20, then 15/15, and so on—as long as there is no huffing and puffing.

Note: There is no goal to reach any amount of running or walking. Find the right strategy that works for you on any given day.

Remember that your muscles, heart, blood system, and mind–body connections can all work as a team if you progress gradually and avoid setbacks. If you have any aches, pains, or lingering fatigue, drop back to a more comfortable ratio and treat the area if there is possible damage. Tell your doctor about any medical issues that could indicate issues from your injury.

Read the last situation on TMS, if you have pains. Pain generated by TMS can be managed in most cases while you continue to train. Always consult a doctor who wants you to continue to run if you suspect there is significant damage that requires layoff. Stay below the threshold of irritation when there is damage.

Don't allow your reflex brain to take control and stimulate negative hormones. These trigger thoughts such as, "You used to be in such great shape," "This is baby stuff, you can push yourself today," or "You'll never get back to your former fitness level."

Instead, talk back to the reflex brain to shift control to the frontal lobe:

"I'm getting back in shape."

"I feel good about myself."

"I have overcome an injury and am a smarter runner now."

"Speed is not important—it's the joy from each run that keeps me going."

Quick strategies:

» Put a date on a calendar—your mission is to finish a 5K, 10K, half, or full marathon.

» Make a commitment to join a group that runs at your ability level.
» Get a friend to stay in touch with you as you get in shape. Email, text, and call one another as needed.
» Say to yourself when the motivation starts to drop: "I can do it, I can do it!"
» Believe in yourself.

Positive affirmations at the start of a downturn keep you in the executive brain which can stimulate positive peptides locking into receptor molecules, sending positive messages toward an emotional comeback. For more information on positive affirmations, read the chapter, Mantras.

10.7 COMING BACK FROM AN ILLNESS

Don't run if you have a lung infection. A virus in the lungs can move into the heart and cause serious damage. When there is a significant infection, get permission from a doctor who wants you to get back into running as soon as you can. When permission is given, start with a 10-minute walk and always walk or run with a relatively short stride, feet low to the ground. Every other day, extend the walk by three to five minutes until you reach 30 minutes. Then, insert a 5- to 10-second jog every minute into your walk. If this is too much for you at first, walk continuously when needed. Don't do any running the day after you have inserted running segments into your walk to rest the running muscles.

Your goal is to finish each run-walk feeling like you could continue for another 10 minutes or more without any huffing and puffing. When you feel comfortable at a 5- to 10-second run/60-second walk for 30 minutes, extend the time by 5 minutes on one day every other weekend until you reach an hour. On the shorter weekend, stay at 30 to 40 minutes. Shift to doing two other runs a week (usually Tuesday and Thursday) and increase the amount of running. When 10/50 feels too easy on the shorter runs, move up to 10/40. After three to six of these workouts, shift to 10/30. You could either stay at one of those strategies or continue to gradually increase to 15/30, then 15/20, then 15/15, and so on—as long as there is no huffing and puffing.

Note: Don't feel compelled to do more every workout. Find a ratio that works and feels comfortable.

There are a lot of issues in coming back from an illness. Even when you feel somewhat normal, living a sedentary life, the body may not have repaired itself completely. Remember that your muscles, heart, blood system, and mind–body connections can all work as a team if you progress gradually and avoid setbacks. If you have any aches, pains, or lingering fatigue, drop back to a more comfortable ratio and treat the area if there is possible injury. If you suspect that there are medical issues concerning your recovery from the illness, check with your doctor.

Read the last situation on TMS if you have pains. Pain generated by TMS can be managed in most cases while you continue to train. You may need to get your doctor to evaluate whether there is damage in the area that could be increased by running. Stay below the threshold of irritation of a real damaged area.

Don't allow your reflex brain to take control and stimulate negative hormones. These trigger thoughts such as, "You used to be in such great shape," "This is baby stuff, you can push yourself today," or "You'll never get back to your former fitness level."

Instead, talk back to the reflex brain to shift control to the frontal lobe:

"I'm getting back in shape."

"I feel good about myself."

"I have overcome an injury and am a smarter runner now."

"Speed is not important—it's the joy from each run that keeps me going."

Quick strategies:
» Put a date on a calendar—your mission is to finish a 5K, 10K, half, or full marathon.
» Make a commitment to join a group that runs at your ability level.
» Get a friend to stay in touch with you as you get in shape. Email, text, and call one another when needed.
» Say to yourself when the motivation starts drop, "I can do it, I can do it!"
» Believe in yourself.
» Positive affirmations at the start of a downturn keep you in the executive brain which can stimulate positive peptides locking into receptor molecules, sending positive messages toward an emotional comeback. For more information on positive affirmations, read the chapter, Mantras.

10.8 COMING BACK FROM AN EXTENDED LAYOFF

If you have not run for two weeks or more, assume that you have lost all of your conditioning. The good news is that you can regain the fitness you had in less time than it took originally by conservatively increasing your running according to the following plan. If there are medical issues, get permission from a doctor who wants to help you return to running as soon as you can. When there are no issues, start with a 10- to 15-minute walk, and always walk or run with a relatively short stride, feet low to the ground. Every other day, extend the walk by three to five minutes until you reach 30 minutes. Then insert a 10-second jog every minute into your walk. If this is too much for you at first, walk continuously when needed. Only run every other day to rest the running muscles.

Your goal is to finish each run-walk feeling like you could continue for another 10 minutes or more without any huffing and puffing. When you feel comfortable at a 5- to 10-second run/60-second walk for 30 minutes, extend the time by 5 minutes one day a week (usually the weekend) every other weekend until you reach an hour. On the shorter weekend, stay at 30 to 40 minutes. Shift to doing two other runs a week (usually Tuesday and Thursday) and increase the amount of running. When 10/50 feels too easy on the shorter runs, move up to 10/40. After three to six of these workouts, shift to 10/30. You could either stay at one of those strategies or continue to gradually increase to 15-30, then 15/20, then 15/15, and so on—as long as there is no huffing and puffing.

There are a lot of individual issues in coming back from an extended layoff. Above all, find some joy in every run. Don't push too far beyond current limits. Remember that your muscles, heart, blood system, and mind–body connections can all work as a team if you progress gradually and avoid setbacks. If you have any aches, pains, or lingering fatigue, drop back to a more comfortable ratio and treat the area if there is possible damage. If you suspect that there are medical issues during your comeback, check with your doctor.

Read the last situation on TMS if you have pains. Pain generated by TMS can be managed in most cases while you continue to train. You may need to get you doctor to evaluate whether there is damage in the area that could be aggravated by running. Stay below the threshold of irritation of a real damaged area. Most of these aches are temporary and are not cause for alarm.

Don't allow your reflex brain to take control and stimulate negative hormones. These trigger thoughts such as, "You used to be in such great shape," "This is baby stuff, you can push yourself today," or "You'll never get back to your former fitness level."

Instead, talk back to the reflex brain to shift control to the frontal lobe:

"I'm getting back in shape."

"I feel good about myself."

"I have overcome an injury and am a smarter runner now."

"Speed is not important—it's the joy from each run that keeps me going."

Quick strategies:
» Put a date on a calendar—your mission is to finish a 5K, 10K, half, or full marathon.
» Make a commitment to join a group that runs at your ability level.
» Get a friend to stay in touch with you as you get in shape. Email, text, and call one another when needed.
» Say to yourself when the motivation starts to drop, "I can do it, I can do it!"
» Believe in yourself.

Positive affirmations at the start of a downturn keep you in the executive brain which can stimulate positive peptides locking into receptor molecules, sending positive messages toward an emotional comeback. For more information on positive affirmations, read the chapter, Mantras.

10.9 COMING BACK AFTER A BAD WORKOUT OR RACE

All runners have bad days. The most prominent factor that sets a champion apart from others is the ability to move forward after a setback. Spend a few minutes trying to learn what you may have done that brought on the problem, and you will improve in many ways. Read the chapter, Injury Troubleshooting, for solutions to common problems. These are cognitive actions and will keep the executive brain in charge.

If you don't activate the conscious brain, the subconscious brain will sense stress from the setback and stimulate negative hormones. These can trigger negative messages such as, "You are losing it," "Running isn't fun anymore," "You'll never get to your goal," and "Why are you doing this?" If you focus on these and believe them, you will allow the reflex brain to create negative feelings, stimulate negative peptides, and lower your motivation. Here are some steps for turning your attitude in a positive direction.

1. **Re-establish the joy of running.** Take several easy runs with enough walk breaks to leave you feeling good from the beginning. Don't set any time goal for these runs. The positive hormones will start the shift to a good attitude.

2. **Ignore negative messages.** Counter these with positive mantras: "I love to run," "I can improve," and "I'm in control."

3. **List the mistakes or causes of the bad run**—and what you will do to prevent future situations.

4. **Deal with significant unresolved issues (specific mistakes made by you or others) at the beginning of the run.** Vent and get this frustration, rage, and anger out of your system. Let it go.

5. **State one positive aspect of the problem run.**

6. **Come up with a plan for the next run.**

7. **Believe in the plan.**

10.10 BURNING FAT

It is possible to burn fat without running 100 miles a week or being hungry all the time. The secret: staying focused on running and walking and using your conscious brain when you choose foods at mealtimes. Be sure to read the next chapter, Cognitive Control Over Nutrition—Fat Burning.

Our subconscious brain has numerous eating patterns that reward us for eating. In *The End of Overeating*, Dr. David Kessler explains how eating various combinations of sugar, salt, and fat triggers the neurotransmitter dopamine which delivers a temporary dose of joy. Such *comfort food experiences* that are often repeated become hardwired into the reflex brain as a stimulus–response activity. So when we are talking to friends at a party with a bowl of potato chips nearby, it is common to subconsciously eat one after another without being aware of doing so. The taste of each is so rewarding that we can't stop at one—or 20—because we allow the subconscious brain to be in charge. No accountability.

Concepts of fat burning:
» Aerobic running burns fat. Liberal walk breaks help you stay aerobic.
» Long, aerobic runs can adapt the muscle cells to be better fat burners.
» During speed training and fast running, you're not burning fat, but glycogen (stored form of carbohydrate). So slower is better for fat burning.
» Walking is aerobic—the more steps you take, the more fat you burn without a significant hunger response.
» Monitor food intake by using one of the programs or websites that give you accountability.

Tools that can help you shift away from monkey brain eating:
1. Use a website like www.fitday.com to monitor intake and analyze nutrition.
2. Use a resource like *Running and Fatburning for Women* by Barbara and Jeff Galloway or *Nutrition for Runners* by Jeff Galloway with Nancy Clark RDN.
3. for additional information to help understand the process better.
4. Set your calorie deficit goal each day (150-350 calories).
5. Set up a calorie budget for each day (websites and apps can help you with tracking).
6. Get a step counter and increase the number of walking steps to achieve your calorie deficit (10,000 is the goal).

7. As you monitor your eating and exercise, your conscious brain is in control. You can then take action to improve efficiency of the process. You control your budget.

8. By increasing walking steps to more than 10,000, you can eat a few more calories and still lose fat if you set up and follow the calorie budget.

How to modify reflex eating behaviors:

» Estimate calorie content before eating anything—this shifts consciousness to frontal lobe.

» If there are foods that you really love that are hazardous to your diet, eat small amounts and account for each.

» Search for foods that are healthy that you can gradually swap for the hazardous foods.

» Reward yourself for making progress with non-food items.

10.11 WHEN A CLOSE RUNNING FRIEND MOVES AWAY

The loss of a faithful running companion is stressful to the subconscious brain and results in lower motivation to run. When a running dog dies, for example, many runners lose motivation and cut themselves off from the good peptides that could turn their attitude around. A cognitive strategy can restart the program.

If a running companion moves away, call him or her before a run. Talking and hearing the voice can recharge many of the positive motivational peptides that can get you out the door. Many runners actually bring a cellphone with them and call when the motivation runs low. Some call this their *lifeline* or *motivation connection.*

Go to races, talk to other runners in your neighborhood, and attend running club meetings. Look for running groups, such as the Galloway programs. Most runners who reach out for another running buddy find one.

Stay in touch with your friend, and run together in a mutually agreed upon race. This turns on the positive attitude brain circuits with more vitality.

You realize that running alone activates the same good brain effects you experienced when running with your buddy and keeps the positive attitude peptides transmitting good messages.

10.12 MANAGING TENSION MYOSITIS SYNDROME (TMS)

Dr. John Sarno is an orthopedist who practiced traditional medicine for years. Then he discovered a condition called tension myositis syndrome (TMS), as well as the methods for treating it. This dramatically improved his cure rate. I recommend his books *The Mindbody Prescription: Healing the Body, Healing the Pain* and *Healing Back Pain: The Mind-Body Connection* because they have helped thousands of people to manage or eliminate chronic pain and get on with their running and their lives.

A runner who is experiencing TMS is allowing the subconscious brain to monitor stress. To shift control to the conscious brain at the beginning of a workout, it helps to identify sources of stress and talk them out or just vent as you're moving down the road. Dr. Sarno says that you don't have to resolve an issue to manage or cure the pain. You just need to be aware of it and then take some conscious action to move control away from the reflex brain.

Sarno explains how inner stress build-up activates TMS. The reflex brain receives the continuous information flow through the peptide network, which identifies the areas of the body that have been damaged.

When the total stress level rises significantly, the reflex brain reduces blood flow to these areas, dramatically increasing pain. But when a person takes conscious control over the reflex brain by deciding to do things such as talk to the reflex brain, the blood flow can be restored, and TMS can be managed. Here are some statements that have worked:

"I know what you are doing, reflex brain, and I won't allow it."

"Open up the flow in my_____."

"I'm in control here."

"I'm not going to let the reflex brain control the blood flow."

Note: When there is pain, get guidance from your doctor before running to ensure that running or walking will not make the condition worse. It's best to be under the care of a doctor who understands TMS and wants you to run if you can.

10.13 REPROGRAMMING THE MONKEY BRAIN TO USE RUN WALK RUN

Most children, at some time, have been instructed in physical education class or on a sports team to never walk. A common coaching statement that is embedded in the reflex brain is "walking is failure." There are reasons why coaches will instruct their students to keep running during short events. But it is not necessary to follow this advice for the rest of our lives.

It's a fact that this childhood programming is very powerful. When we start to take a walk break, even 20 years after we finished our last cross-country race or PE class, stress builds up in the reflex brain, and anxiety hormones are produced—because you are taking an action that goes counter to the programming in the reflex brain. The reflex brain may also trigger your memory to remind you what your coach said (or at least a fuzzy remembrance).

But there's hope. We can take charge over this and other hardwired subconscious patterns by following these steps. As you repeat this strategy on every run, you can reprogram the reflex brain to accept taking walking breaks as normal.

1. Use the magic mile to determine a realistic goal pace and a conservative long-run pace.
2. Set the run walk run ratio based upon the pace per mile of both the goal pace and the long-run pace, using the chapter, The Galloway Run Walk Run Method, as a guide.
3. Read the chapter, and learn all the key phrases. Memorize these or write them down so that you can talk back to the reflex brain's negative messages:
   > Walk breaks make me strong to the end.
   > Walk breaks allow me to do what I want to the rest of the day.
   > Walk breaks speed my recovery.
   > Walk breaks help me run faster.
   > Walk breaks let me control fatigue.
   > Walk breaks break up the distance into doable segments.
   > Walk breaks give me control over my running enjoyment.

4. Get a run walk run timer or program your watch for segments. The $20 timer is available on my website, jeffgalloway.com. It will get you into a rhythmical pattern of run walk run. This is a great way to reprogram the reflex brain.

5. At the end of each run, make a conscious statement about how the Run Walk Run Method is superior to your old way: "I have a tool to enjoy running for life."

YOU DETERMINE HOW MUCH YOU RUN AND HOW MUCH YOU WALK

One of the wonderful aspects of running is that there is no definition of a *runner* that you must live up to. There are also no rules that you must follow as you do your daily run. You are the captain of your running ship, and it is you who determines how far, how fast, how much you will run and walk. Walk breaks can keep the first-time runner from injury and burnout and can help veterans to improve time. While you will hear many opinions on this, running has always been a freestyle type of activity in which *each individual is empowered to mix and match the many variables* and come out with the running experience that he or she chooses.

11 COGNITIVE CONTROL OVER NUTRITION—FAT BURNING

USE YOUR CONSCIOUS BRAIN TO MANAGE ADEQUATE NUTRITION, HUNGER, CRAVINGS, ENERGY, FATIGUE, AND FAT

As humans, we can activate our conscious brain to

» avoid mindless eating by managing our nutrition,

» ensure we are getting adequate nutrients,

» enjoy food without adding extra layers of fat, and

» combine mind and body to achieve our goals.

All of us are capable of using our conscious brains to control what we eat. In the process we discover far more joy throughout the mind–body network from making healthy food choices and exercising than we did eating potato chips or hot wings on the couch.

I also hear from thousands of talented runners every year who tell me that they tried to eat better but relapsed back into the comfort foods containing sugar salt and fat that don't deliver the nutrients needed for repair and performance. Some are not overweight and some are running quite well. I tell them in the short run they may not notice a difference when they transition to healthier choices. Long term health and well-being will improve with good nutrition.

I've heard from thousands who have not had the performance capacity to stay ahead of the pick-up bus in their favorite marathon or qualify for the Boston Marathon but found that a healthy dietary change became a catalyst during their improvement journey. Because they felt better with more energy, the workouts were better—especially on the tough days. A positive change in food choices has been shown to turn on brain circuits to improve quality in exercise.

By using the simple strategies in this book you can set up a cognitive eating plan that will put you in command of your food intake and will make you feel better every day. This can significantly improve the way you feel when running and performing your daily activities. When you combine aerobic, enjoyable running with mental focus on eating, you can feel better, prepare for improved performance, reduce general fatigue, recover faster, and burn more fat.

We have a powerful mind–body network that is interconnected. Eating influences mental activity, and mental activity influences eating—all day long. But we have many subconscious eating patterns that are deeply embedded. This chapter details the exciting new research, showing how you can consciously activate brain circuits to give you control over subconscious eating patterns that lower our energy and reduce motivation for running.

Yes, you can harness this network to be the master of your nutrition, feel better, and improve health while controlling diet, weight, and performance nutrition.

11.1 WHO'S IN CHARGE: CONSCIOUS BRAIN OR SUBCONSCIOUS REFLEX BRAIN?

At any given moment, you can choose one of two brain operating systems: 1) the more ancient subconscious brain located in the brainstem or 2) the conscious brain (or human brain) located in the frontal lobe.

The challenge: Subconscious brain gratification eating patterns. Most humans, most of the time, allow the subconscious reflex brain to choose what and when to eat. This is natural because the subconscious brain conducts most of our activities throughout the day. Hardwired in this ancient and continuously upgraded brainstem are thousands of genetically embedded and learned behavior patterns that evolved millions of years ago in response to the constant threat of starvation. To enhance survival, our subconscious brain developed many circuits that stimulate us to eat much more food than we need whenever food is available, while stimulating hormones that make us feel good when we eat sugar and fat. Brain circuits keep rewarding us with a joy hormone called dopamine even when we've eaten far more than we need for the next day or two—without feeling satisfied.

Overeating can compromise goals, even for skinny runners: Even if you don't need or want to lose weight, subconscious eating patterns can cause gastrointestinal issues that may keep you from your goals. The simple cognitive eating plans in this book can help you make the best choices before and after workouts and races so that you can perform at your best.

Use your conscious brain and gain control over eating: You can take control of your nutritional destiny by having a cognitive strategy for eating. This shifts control out of the subconscious brain and into the frontal lobe. As you focus on what you eat, how much, and when, the conscious brain overrides the subconscious brain. This interrupts embedded emotional subconscious eating patterns and gives you a chance to choose foods that will keep you energized and healthy, while you avoid overeating. By having an eating plan, you can combine the foods you need to balance your nutrients, keep the energy supply flowing, and avoid dehydration.

You don't have to give up the foods you love. But whether you want to ensure that you're getting the right nutrients for health and strong running or whether you want to burn some fat, an eating strategy will allow you to achieve your goals for eating and running.

How subconscious monkey brain circuits work

1. **Subconscious brain circuits are set up to eat when food is available.** Most of the energy and eating circuits were developed over millions of years when food was scarce and starvation was common. For survival, our appetite circuit is turned on when food is available and is not turned off until we have eaten far more than we need for that day and often the next day or two (i.e., a visit to the buffet). The extra volume not only promotes fat accumulation as a hedge against starvation, but a wealth of vitamins, minerals, and protein for repair and body function.

2. **Subconscious dopamine reflex eating means no accountability.** Many of the subconscious reflex brain eating patterns are not healthy or beneficial for running. Take the dopamine reflex reward pattern, for example. Dopamine is a neurotransmitter—a hormone that delivers a more powerful sense of joy than most. When you eat a food that has sugar, salt, or fat, such as a potato chip (which has all three), you get a happy dose of dopamine, making you feel so good. But the feeling is gone so fast that you reach for another and then another. If you choose to stay under the control of the monkey brain, there is no accountability as you pile on the calories. Such eating patterns produced greater fat storage by our ancestors, which gave them a chance to make it through the weeks when food was not available. You'll find out more about this in my book, *Nutrition for Runners*.

3. **Stress stimulates subconscious eating patterns.** When we allow it to be in control, the subconscious brain will monitor overall stress. As stress level increases to what the brain determines to be overload, the subconscious brain will trigger the release of anxiety and negative attitude hormones. One of the most common circuits that is activated to counter this stress and negative attitude build-up is the dopamine reflex. The simple subconscious fix is to reach for sugar, salt, or fat and feel better quick (but only temporarily). Many runners justify carbohydrate loading by subconsciously snacking to counter the stress of an upcoming race or long run.

MONKEY BRAIN SNACKING BUILDS FAT

When stressed or very tired, it is common to subconsciously reach for sugary, salty, or fatty snacks to get a dose of dopamine. Unfortunately the reward is very temporary, leading to multiple doses with no accountability. The way you can gain control is to have a strategy. See my books, *Running and Fat Burning for Women and Nutrition for Runners,* for more strategies for accountable eating.

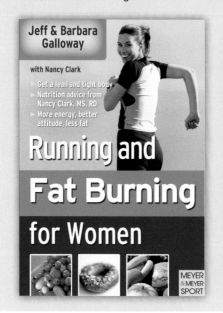

4. **Subconscious brain eating patterns can lead to addictive eating behaviors.** Dr. Pam Peeke, in her book, *The Hunger Fix*[9], has noted the research showing how addictive eating patterns can damage the natural reward centers of the brain so that more and more junk food is needed for gratification. Ultimately there is no satisfaction and less and less dopamine when large amounts are ingested. She has also identified a "detox program" with exercise and eating plans that have helped thousands to enjoy eating healthy food. Here are some of the many insightful tips from this book:

    › A diet full of unhealthy fat, salt, and sugar switches on certain genes to cope.

    › As one savors sugar, histones direct genes to increase insulin.

    › Increased insulin with excess unhealthy sugar calorie intake increases fat storage.

---

9   Peeke, P. 2013. *The Hunger Fix*. Emmaus: Rodale Books

> Regular, repeated ingestions and insulin secretions can result in insulin resistance and type 2 diabetes.
> Too much food intake stimulates the creation of fat cells.
> Higher levels of fat trigger hormones that increase pain in joints and "weak links."

Energy is the first priority. Forward movement kept our ancient ancestors alive—the more territory covered the more food gathering possibilities. Maintaining energy is top priority throughout the mind–body network, and there are many effective brain circuits that keep the energy flowing even when there are challenges.

The brain's only fuel is blood glucose. When the supply of blood sugar is adequate, the brain will keep the many complex systems going, including an adequate energy system required for muscles to do their work. If we don't eat regularly and the blood sugar level is lowered, the brain will start reducing blood flow to key areas, tuning down metabolism energy level, reducing brain function, and shutting things down.

Fat is the backup fuel. We are hardwired to store fat for survival. Numerous internal circuits connect mind and body to ensure energy supply when food supply is below current energy needs or unavailable (i.e., periods of starvation). The brain circuit commonly called *set point* maintains and monitors fat storage, as well as triggers an increase in appetite when set point is low and food is available. When on a dramatic calorie reduction, fat is released. Set point has memory, however. When returning to normal eating levels after losing 30 pounds due to a continued starvation diet, for example, the set point stimulates hunger a bit more, day after day, until the set point of fat from before the diet is added—often with a few additional pounds around the waistline.

» The crucial role of regular aerobic exercise—Your energy supply system is designed to adapt to regular aerobic exercise. Exercising about every other day will keep these circuits in good operation, while the executive brain searches for more efficient ways of eating, repairing, storing, and burning.

» In most workouts, intensity should be low for fat burning and appetite management. Workouts need to be aerobic, meaning no huffing and puffing.

» By adjusting the amounts of running and walking, you can reduce the intensity and stress, staying in the aerobic zone—the fat burning zone.

» Gentle aerobic running stimulates production of BDNF—miracle grow for the brain and nerves and also important for memory, learning, critical thinking, and decision making.

» The meditative effect of a gentle run-walk can help in the healing of dopamine damage from addictive eating patterns (Peeke, 2013).

» Anaerobic exercise (working hard so that you are huffing and puffing) doesn't burn fat, shuts down digestive blood flow, reduces ability to reload within 30 minutes, and stimulates hunger.

» Once you burn a threshold of calories each day (usually 700-900 calories), the appetite circuit tends to curb hunger.

The satisfaction circuit—The hunger reduction brain circuit is turned on by reaching a threshold of calories burned each day. The amount needed is between 700 and 900 calories from all sources, according to Portman and Ivy in their book, *Hardwired for Fitness*. So for those wanting to lose weight and burn fat, gentle exercise in the morning can give them a head start on managing appetite for the rest of the day.

The good attitude circuit—It is well established that running activates your good attitude better than just about anything you can do. Run gently, turn on a good attitude, and you will be less susceptible to dopamine eating.

The vitality circuit—Thousands of runners have reported experiences similar to the following: "Arriving home after a long day, I often feel too tired with no energy to exercise. The run was scheduled, but there seemed to be no resources to run for a minute or two, and 30 minutes seemed impossible. Promising myself that I would only go for 5 minutes, I got out the door. Surprisingly, the energy started flowing. Day after day I have to break my promise, running 30, 45, 60 minutes with no problems. Often I had more energy afterward than was experienced all day long and did many more projects that evening than was the norm."

Running at the right pace from the beginning (with the right ratio of walk breaks) activates the vitality circuit. This often reduces the craving and intake of snacks normally done to boost blood sugar levels (BSL) on a stressful day. But most runners I've coached in this area tell me they need a series of healthy snacks during the day to keep boosting the BSL.

The empowerment circuit—Finishing a run, especially on a tough day, turns on the empowerment circuit, which can give you the mental control to take care of your eating and your life. Running tends to activate the conscious brain which overrides the monkey brain. When running regularly, runners tell me that they feel more motivated to change their diet for the better.

11.2 TOOLS THAT GIVE YOU CONTROL OVER NUTRITION

We have all of the mental power needed to gain control over our food choices and quantity. This allows us to eat the foods we like while ensuring the intake of vital nutrients. By using the powerhouse in our frontal lobe, we can gain control over fat levels by focusing on a plan for eating and exercise.

But we often defer control to the subconscious monkey brain. It is embedded with dozens of powerful eating circuits that were designed to help our ancestors survive the constant periods of starvation.

The monkey brain is programmed to keep eating when food is available—long after we have eaten enough nutrition for the next 24 hours. It will also lead us to choose foods that taste good, triggering an ancient circuit that craves the next hit of dopamine from the junk foods, potato chip after potato chip. Because the subconscious is in control, there is no accountability.

But you can take control by choosing the brain component that you want to use every time you decide to eat something. Deciding will activate the conscious brain. If you have a cognitive eating strategy, you can control what goes in your mouth, maintain energy and blood sugar level, balance nutritional elements, and avoid fat increase. This is frontal lobe eating with accountability. You are in charge!

You don't have to eat a large quantity of food to get the right balance of nutrients. You simply need to engage your conscious brain and do the accounting.

1. Write everything down that you eat: food, amount, ingredients.
2. Enter your data into a website or app.
3. Analyze your results every day or two.

All of these steps activate the frontal lobe so that you are in control. As you do this regularly, you will shift to conscious brain control as you consider something to eat. Most runners who have done this tell me that they have progressively chosen healthier choices and reduced the junk dopamine choices.

You will learn more about how and why fat is deposited in *Nutrition for Runners* and *Running and Fat Burning for Women*. For now, realize that starvation was a major cause of death until recent times, and there are significant brain networks to ensure that we maintain fat levels that are usually higher than we consciously want them to be. The sections on fat burning in both books also explain how conscious control over eating and exercise can often help you adjust the fat level on your body.

By using the frontal lobe, you can set up an eating strategy, monitor intake, and ensure adequate intake of vitamins, minerals, and protein. This means that you will focus on each issue several times a day and set up your plan to stay on track—and away from monkey brain control.

COGNITIVE EATING

1. Determine the number of pounds you want to lose.
2. Set up a calorie budget to achieve a 200 to 500 calorie deficit per day.
3. Write down everything you eat and look at the totals at least once a day.
4. Add walking steps to your day by using a step counter, fitbit, or another similar device.
5. Make adjustments as needed to stay on track every day.

YOU ARE THE CAPTAIN OF YOUR EATING SHIP!

12 COGNITIVE CONTROL OVER INJURIES

Knowledge gives you the power to avoid injuries. Once you understand the major cause of injuries and are consciously monitoring early warning signs and taking action, you can avoid the downtime.

What causes injuries?

Our bodies are programmed to adapt to running and walking by making constant upgrades to withstand stress and perform more efficiently. My training plans offer a series of components, cognitively arranged in sequence. Regular, small increases in workload stimulate improvements followed by recovery periods to promote rebuilding and improved capacity. The factor that is most commonly neglected is rest, but it is crucial.

Note: It is during the recovery period that the rebuilding takes place.

Each of us has a few weak links that take on more stress when we work out. These are the areas that ache, hurt, don't work correctly when we start a new activity or increase training, or don't provide sufficient rest after a hard workout. In some cases, pain-killing hormones, such as endorphins, will mask the damage. Most commonly, exercisers go into denial, ignore the first signs of irritation, and keep training until the stressed area breaks down.

To sustain progress and avoid injury, we simply need to focus, write down the training plan, follow it, and make changes when needed.

» A slight increase in training produces a minor breakdown of tissue.
» If the post-workout rest period is sufficient, the muscles, tendons, and cardiovascular system will rebuild to handle a higher level of performance.
» All body parts continue to adapt in structure, efficiency, and performance when there is a balance between workout stress and rest.

Be sensitive to your weak links

Most of the aches and pains experienced by my runners and walkers are located in their weak link areas—the muscles, joints, and tendons that take more stress due to our individual range of motion and workload. If you will stay focused on the irritation of a key area and take action, you may avoid the downtime due to injuries.

Common weak links:

» Joints—knee, hip, ankle
» Muscles—calf, hamstring, quadriceps
» Tendons—Achilles, knee, ankle
» Fascia—especially around joints, foot
» Bones—foot and leg
» Nerve tissue—foot and leg
» Feet—just about any area can be overstressed

Cognitive Hint: Make a list of your weak links in your journal and check each one every day.

There is often no sensation of pain during or immediately after the workout because the body has a number of pain-killing mechanisms, including endorphins, which will temporarily mask the symptoms of isolated microtears in muscles and tendons or inflammation in joints. But when a critical mass of these broken fibers or inflammation has accumulated in one area, you have produced more damage than the body can repair in 48 hours—you have an injury.

Common causes of injuries

It's a physiological fact that the constant use of a muscle, tendon, or joint without a break will result in earlier fatigue and reduced work potential. This is why non-stop running increases injury risk dramatically. Continuing to run when the muscle is extremely fatigued increases the quantity of microtears dramatically and is a major cause of injury.

Take cognitive action!

» Use a journal—the best tool to keep you in the executive brain (read the chapter, Your Journal Gives You Cognitive Control Over Training).

» Evaluate your pacing every day.

» Long runs should be run 3 minutes per mile slower than current half marathon race pace or 4 min/mi slower than current 5K pace.

» Use the right run walk run strategy for the pace currently run.

» Adjust pace for heat, recent sickness, or layoff.

» Take more rest days per week if needed.

» When running speedwork, ensure the pace matches current ability and provide rest between repetitions.

» Slow down 30 seconds per mile for every 5 degrees above 60 °F when it's hot.

Note: Studies show that runners have healthier joints and fewer orthopedic complaints than non-runners after decades of running. See the third edition of my book, *Running Until You're 100*, for more information.

Focus on running form

» **Stride length**—Longer strides increase risk. A shorter stride may not slow you down if you will increase cadence or turnover.

» **Bounce off the ground**—The higher the bounce, the more stress on the push-off muscles. The higher the bounce, the more shock to be absorbed upon landing. Stay low to the ground, touching lightly.

» **Stretching**—I have heard from thousands of runners who have been injured or had injuries aggravated by stretching. In general, I do not recommend stretching. There are individuals who benefit from certain stretches, however. Be careful if you choose to stretch. Stretching is not generally recommended as a warm-up or immediately after running. Trying to stretch out fatigue-induced tightness often results in injury or prolonged recovery. If you do stretch, it's best to do it after the muscles have been properly warmed up.

How do you know if you are injured?

Continuing to exercise when you feel that you might have an injury puts you at great risk for an extended layoff from running. In most cases that I've monitored, when I suspect that there is an injury, it usually is an injury. Be sensitive to your weak links. Focus on the following three signs. If you notice any of the symptoms, take at least a day or two off from running.

» **Inflammation**—swelling, puffiness, or thickening
» **Loss of function**—the area doesn't work correctly or move normally
» **Pain**—if the pain does not go away as you get warmed up and walk slowly, or the pain increases, STOP!

Taking days off from running

You can take five days off from running with no significant loss in conditioning. It is always better to err on the conservative side of injury repair. If you take an extra day off at the beginning of an injury, you won't lose any conditioning. But if you continue training with an injury, you may increase the healing time by a week or a month for each day you try to push through pain.

Quick action can reduce recovery time needed

Some minor irritation may require just one day off from running. As the pain level increases, so does the need for more recovery days because there is usually more damage.

How to lower the chance of injury:

» Work out every other day (lowest rate of injury).
» Insert walk breaks and shuffle breaks into your runs or walks.
» Avoid faster running or gently ease into faster running.
» Don't stretch (unless you have certain stretches that work for you and don't hurt you).

Reducing the risk of speed injuries:

» Warm up. Start very slowly and then gradually increase some accelerations, easing into the workout.

» Run the first and the last repetition more slowly than the others.

» Rest between repetitions. If you have a history of speed injuries, take more rest.

» Take walk breaks during the repetitions. During a mile repetition workout, for example, take half of the amount of walking you plan to take during the marathon itself.

Focus on form

While the body adapts and adjusts to the running motion, workouts or races that are long and strenuous can result in irregularities in our normal form. Since the body is not adapted to these wobbles, weak links can be irritated. Continued use—using an unaccustomed range of motion—can lead to injury. Here are some of the common ones. For more information see my books *Half-Marathon: You Can Do It, 5K/10K Running.*

TROUBLESHOOTING FORM-RELATED INJURIES

Lower back—Caused by forward lean, overstriding, and too few walk breaks

Neck pain—Caused by forward lean with head placed too far forward or back

Hamstring pain—Caused by striding too long and stretching

Shin pain on front—Caused by striding too long, especially on downhills or at end of run

Shin pain on inside—Caused by overpronation

Achilles tendon pain—Caused by stretching, speedwork, and overpronation

Calf pain—Caused by stretching, speedwork, and inadequate number of walk breaks

Knee pain—Caused by too few walk breaks and overpronation

The shuffle

The most efficient and gentle running form is a *shuffle*. The feet stay next to the ground, touching lightly with a relatively short stride. When running at the most relaxed range of the shuffling motion, the ankle mechanism does a great deal of the work, and little effort is required from the calf muscle. But when the foot pushes harder and bounces more and the stride increases, there are often more aches, pains, and injuries.

Correct posture reduces aches and pains

Research shows that upright posture results in the most efficient form. It can also reduce stress on weak links. Most of the runners I've worked with find that an upright posture (like a puppet on a string) is best in all ways. When runners use a forward lean, there is a tendency to develop lower-back pain and neck pain. A small minority of runners naturally run with a forward lean with no problems. Run the way that is most natural.

Suggestions for running smoother to reduce irritation to weak links:

» Feet should be low to the ground. Use a light foot touch.

» Try not to bounce more than an inch off the ground.

» Let your feet move the way that is natural for them. If you tend to land on your heel and roll forward, do so.

» If you have motion control issues, a foot device can provide minor correction to bring you into alignment and avoid irritating a weak link. A supportive shoe may also be needed.

» Maintain a gentle stride that allows your leg muscles to stay relaxed. In general, it's better to have a shorter stride and focus on quicker turnover if you want to speed up.

» Water running can help in eliminating flips and turns of the feet and legs which sometimes cause injuries, aches, or pains. With a flotation device, run in the deep end of the pool so that your foot does not touch the bottom. Even one session of 15 minutes once a week can be beneficial.

12.1 EXERCISES THAT CAN PREVENT AND TREAT INJURIES

Toe squincher—For plantar fascia and foot injuries

This strengthens the many muscles in the foot, promoting a strong push-off, reducing foot fatigue, and reducing foot damage. Point your foot down and contract the muscles of the foot, curling the toes in. Keep the contraction until the foot cramps. This can be done either wearing shoes or barefoot. Repeat 15 to 20 times a day.

Arm running—For back and shoulder soreness and pain

Holding dumbbells in each hand, go through a slightly exaggerated motion you would use when running for a set of 10 repetitions (one left and one right equals one repetition).

Pick a weight that is heavy enough so that you feel you have strengthened the shoulder and neck muscles but don't have to struggle to finish the last two repetitions. **Note:** I have a YouTube video showing this exercise.

Foam roller—For IT band injury and pain

This is the only treatment I've found that can speed the healing of the IT band. Use a cylinder of dense foam (illustrated on www.jeffgalloway.com). Lie down on your side, where the IT pain is felt. Rest your body weight on the roller and move your body with your hands so that you're rolling from below the pain site to just above it. Roll for 5 minutes before the run, 5 minutes after the run, and 5 minutes before bed at night (probably the most effective).

The BFF—For any area where you experience pain

This is a vibrating massage tool that brings blood flow to needed areas, speeding recovery. It invigorates muscles and other damaged areas and has helped speed up recovery from long runs and speed workouts. For more info, visit www.jeffgalloway.com.

Ice massage—For pain in the Achilles and other tendons next to the skin

Freeze a paper cup filled with water. Peel off the outer layer at the top to expose part of the ice. Rub the ice constantly over the tendon for 15 minutes. The area should be numb after the treatment.

Night treatments may help the most

Experts tell me that most of the healing occurs overnight. If you perform one of these treatments before you go to bed, you may speed up the healing process.

Preventing speed injuries

Running faster than your comfortable pace for that day will increase injury risk. The farther and faster you go in a speed workout or race, the greater the risk. But since you must run faster during some workouts to run faster in races, here are some ways of reducing this risk.

» Warm up thoroughly:
  1. Walk for 3 minutes.
  2. Then run-walk for 10 minutes, using a lot more walk breaks than you use in a normal run. If you use a 90-second run/30-second walk normally, do the first 10 minutes at a 30/30, 20/20, or 15/15 (run a minute and walk a minute).

3. Next, run for 5 minutes, starting slowly and gradually picking up the pace to a normal short run pace.

4. Finally, do four to eight acceleration gliders: Run for 15 steps at a slow jog and then 15 steps at a faster jog, gradually accelerating to workout pace over 15 steps and then gliding or coasting back down to a jog over 30 to 40 steps. Take a 30- to 60-second walk/jog and repeat. After four to eight of these, walk for 2 to 3 minutes and start the workout or line-up for the race.

» Ease into the speed for the day. Run the first repetition at a pace that is 15 seconds per mile slower than you want to run in the middle of the workout. Run the first mile of your race about 15 to 30 seconds slower than your goal pace for that race.

» Insert walk breaks from the beginning. These will vary based upon pace and race distance or repetition distance. For more information, see my books *Running: Testing Yourself, 5K/10K Running, Half-Marathon: You Can Do It, and Running: A Year Round Plan.*

» Walk to recover between speed repetitions. The amount of walking will vary depending upon the distance of the goal race and the pace. It is better to err on the side of walking longer if you feel the need early on, there are more aches than usual, or the temperature is above 70 °F (14 °C).

» Never run through pain, swelling, or loss of function—stop the workout. After walking for a few minutes, if the pain goes away, resume the workout with caution. If you start to limp in any way, stop.

» Stay smooth even when tired. If your form is changing due to fatigue, slow down.

» Run the last repetition 15 seconds per mile slower than the pace of the middle repetitions.

» Don't run too many speed workouts, races, or other fast runs too close together.

If you focus cognitively on your weak links, take the appropriate walk breaks and rest days, stop training when there could be an injury, and treat a damaged body part, it's possible to avoid all serious injuries. This will bestow the greatest reward from running: enjoyment of every run.

13 TRAINING TOOLS THAT MANAGE AND LOWER WORKOUT STRESS

When workouts and rest are balanced, stress can be managed, reducing a build-up and overload that otherwise would trigger negative peptides, lowering motivation. When you find a way to insert joy into a run, even stressful workouts can leave you feeling positive. Too many hard workouts or challenges that exceed current ability result in lingering fatigue and increased stress. This stimulates production of negative neuropeptides which send their low motivation messages. If corrections are not made, the reflex brain will often reduce blood flow to weak links, the gut, muscles, and the frontal lobe, causing pain, the loss of energy, reduced muscle function, and foggy mental focus.

Here are some proven ways to regain control over your attitude and motivation:

1. Set realistic goals each season. Use the magic mile to set up a leap of faith goal and to monitor improvement. Use the magic mile time trial as a reality check. See page 124.

2. The body responds better to gradual improvement, allowing the many internal systems to improve the infrastructure without being exhausted or breaking down. A 3% performance improvement is realistic during a training season, while a 5% improvement is possible but very challenging. So a modest improvement of 3% every 6 months is more likely to lead to steady and progressive changes over several years. See page 124.

3. The long runs are the most important training component in any training program. They will bestow the endurance necessary for your goal. You cannot go too slowly on the long ones. I recommend running at least 2 minutes per mile slower than your magic mile is predicting in the marathon itself—but it is better to go at a pace that is 3 to 4 minutes per mile slower. For maximum benefit, build the series of long-distance runs beyond the distance of the race, as noted in the schedules in *5K/10K Running, Half-Marathon: You Can Do It, Marathon: You Can Do It, Galloway Training Programs*, and *Running: A Year Round Plan.* By going longer than marathon distance you may never hit the wall again.

4. Be sure to read the chapter on the Galloway Run Walk Run Method. Go with the ratio of running to walking, as noted. It is always OK to take the walk breaks more frequently.

5. Time goal runners: On non-long-run weekends, run a series of speed workouts as noted in *Running: A Year Round Plan, Half-Marathon: You Can Do It, Marathon: You Can Do It,* and *Galloway Training Programs.* These train you to deal with the physical and psychological challenges during the last six miles of your race—where your time goal is either made or compromised. These push back your performance wall—both mentally and physically.

6. Insert sufficient rest between the stress workouts to allow all the body parts to rebuild. Rest is crucial if you want to benefit from the hard workouts instead of increasing the fatigue level or breaking down with injury. On low mileage days, even if you have a form drill or hill workout scheduled, if you feel that you need to jog easily on that day and shorten the mileage, do so.

7. Back off when your gut instinct tells you that you may be getting injured. The prime reason that runners don't achieve their goal is injury interruption with the loss of capacity. When your intuition tells you may have an injury and there are signs of this, stop the workout and take an extra day or two off. Consult with a doctor about medical issues.

8. The cadence drills can reduce mechanical stress by helping you run smoother and more efficiently. These are scheduled into short runs during the week (usually Tuesday and Thursday). See page 148.

9. The acceleration-gliders train the muscles to shift gears when needed so that you're ready for any challenge. They also help you glide to save muscle resources while maintaining speed. See page 149.

10. Hills build just the right amount of strength to deal with hills on your race course. They also help you run more efficiently. See the chapter, Hill Training for Strength and Race Preparation, page 152.

14 REHEARSING THE BIG DAY THE FINAL COUNTDOWN

Mentally rehearsing the goal race is the most effective mental preparation I've found for runners who are approaching a race that challenges them. As you get closer to the deadline on race day, you will sense more stress. Most of the runners I've worked with in this area have noticed some phantom aches and pains during this period that were not felt before or after. Using the drill in the TMS section of this book will help you understand the process.

Have a plan! Almost every runner has some nervous moments during the days and hours leading to the race. If you have a plan and follow it, you can shift control into the frontal lobe and move from one step to the next. Here is a plan that you can customize for your needs and the logistics of your race.

THE AFTERNOON BEFORE

Some like to run a little and some don't run at all the day before the race. You won't lose any conditioning if you take two days off from running leading up to the race. This is a personal issue, and the number of days you do not run before a race is your choice. If you run, think positive thoughts. Say, "I am ready," and, "I can do it."

The carbo-loading dinner

Some events have a dinner the night before. At the dinner you can talk with friends, family members, and other runners. Don't eat foods you haven't eaten before long runs, and don't overeat! Many runners mistakenly assume that they must eat a lot of food the night before. This is actually counterproductive. It generally takes at least 36 hours for the food you eat to be processed and useable in a race—usually longer. It is very unlikely that you will get any significant nutritional help from the "last supper" before the race. Too much *loading* can lead to *unloading* during the event.

THE DAY BEFORE

While you don't want to starve yourself the afternoon and evening before, the best strategy is to eat small meals or snacks that you know are easy for the body to digest, tapering down the amount as you get closer to bedtime. As always, it's best to have done a rehearsal for eating so that you know what works, how much, when to stop eating, and what foods to avoid. Work on your eating plan the evening before each long run, come up with a successful menu, and replicate as you approach race day.

Drinking

The day before, drink 8 glasses (8 oz) of fluid, spread throughout the day, with two of these glasses being a sports drink. Don't drink a lot of fluid during the morning of the race. This can lead to bathroom breaks during the race. Many races have port-a-potties around the start area, but some do not. This is another reason to preview the venue—noting the locations of bathrooms.

Tip: As soon as you wake up, drink a glass of water or a cup of coffee, but then don't drink until the start of the race.

THE NIGHT BEFORE

For those who have had digestive problems during other races, eating is optional after 5pm. If you are hungry, have a light snack that you have tested before and that has not caused problems. Less is better, but don't go to bed with a low blood sugar level. Some can continue to consume small amounts of water or electrolyte beverages (4-6 oz) within the three hours before you go to bed—and some cannot. Avoid alcohol and salty food. Drinking alcohol the night before competition can reduce performance potential. The effects of this central nervous system depressant carry over to the next morning. Alcohol is also a dehydrating agent.

Sleeping

Don't worry if you don't sleep much or at all before your big race. Many runners every year tell me that they run their best times after sleep-deprived nights. Don't keep yourself up on purpose, but if it happens, don't worry about it. It is the worry that stimulates negative attitude hormones and not the lack of sleep.

Pack your bag and lay out your clothes so that you don't have to think very much on race morning. Following are some of the items you should have in your bag:

» Your watch
» Your run walk run timer set for your race-day strategy
» A pace chart, or wrist band, with split times or mile times
» Shoes (with the finish chip attached, if used)
» Socks
» Shorts
» Top—see The Clothing Thermometer
» Outer garment in case of precipitation—can even use a garbage bag with a head hole
» Pin race number on the front of the garment in which you will be finishing
» Bring along a few extra safety pins for your race number (bib number)
» Water, Accelerade, pre-race, and post-race beverages (such as Endurox R4), and a cooler, if you wish
» Food for the drive home
» Bandages, skin lubricant, any other first aid items you may need
» Cash for post-race celebration meal

» A few inspirational thoughts, mantras, jokes, or stories to provide laughs or enter-
  tainment before the start

» Team garments if appropriate

THE MORNING OF THE RACE

Drink 6 to 8 ounces of fluid upon waking. In most cases, this is out of the system before
the start. There will be no nutritional benefit from eating breakfast, but some runners do
it for comfort. Diabetics should follow the advice of their nutritional consultant. Above all,
follow the program that has worked for you before long runs.

RACE-DAY CHECKLIST

Photocopy this list so that you will not only have a plan, you can carry it out in a methodical
and cognitive way. Pack the list in your race bag. Don't try anything new the day of your
race—except for health or safety issues. Stick with your successful plan.

Fluid and potty stops—After you wake up, drink 6 to 8 ounces of water two to three hours
before the start (or use the plan that has worked for you). In order to avoid the bathroom
stops, stop your fluid intake according to your timetable.

Eat what you have eaten before your harder runs. Don't try anything new and avoid
problem foods. It is OK not to eat at all before a race unless you have specific issues
(such as diabetes). If that is the case, then go with the plan that you and your doctor or
nutritionist have worked out.

Get your bearings—Walk around the site to find where you want to line up and how you
will get to the start.

Start your warm-up 20 to 30 minutes before the start—Most marathoners use the first
mile to warm up. You may only walk to get the legs moving, but please, move those legs
for at least 10 minutes of very gentle motion. If possible, go backwards on the course and
preview the start and finish segments for about half a mile each and turn around. This
will give you a preview of the most important parts of your race—start and finish. Use the
warm-up ritual that has worked for you in past workouts and races. Here is a standard
warm-up:

» Walk slowly for 5 to 10 minutes. This may be the only warm-up for non-time goal runners, who may use the first two miles as their gentle warm-up.

» Jog slowly for 10 minutes.

» Over the next 15 to 18 minutes, jog over the start and the finish areas. Visualize starting and finishing.

» Walk around for 3 to 4 minutes.

» **Time goal runners:** Do four to eight acceleration-gliders that gradually increase to the speed you will be running in the race.

» Get in position and focus on the side of the road where you want to go for your walk breaks.

» When runners are called to the start, talk and joke with others. Relax.

Note: Practice this warm-up before one workout every week to get your routine set.

AFTER THE START

Remember that you can control how you feel at the end by being conservative in the beginning.

» Stay with your plan. Take every walk break for the first half of the race at least. If the reflex brain gets anxious as runners pass you, smile and say, "I'll see you folks later." You will!

» Believe in yourself and say, "This is my proven strategy for a strong finish."

» Even if you are pushing fairly hard, enjoy the race as much as possible and smile often.

» On warm days, pour water over your head at the start, possibly wetting your running top.

AT MID-RACE

» When the going gets tough, do everything you can to relax and keep the muscles resilient.

» Keep going—don't give up. Shorten stride and increase turnover, especially when going uphill.

» During the last half mile, don't let your legs slow down. One more step! Success is not letting up. You can do it!

AT THE FINISH

» Your finish is important—you are part of a team of positive runners.

» Keep a quick rhythm—even when very tired.

» Stay in the upright position.

» Cross the finish with a smile on your face.

» You did it!

AFTER THE FINISH

» Keep walking for at least a quarter of a mile.

» Drink about 4 to 8 ounces of fluid.

» Within 30 minutes of the finish, have a snack (100-300 calories) composed of 80% simple carbohydrate and 20% protein (Endurox R4 is best). If this is not available, choose a simple carbohydrate snack.

» If you can soak your legs in cool water during the first two hours after the race, do so (cool water faucet water—ice is not necessary).

» Walk or jog for 20 to 30 minutes later in the day.

» Celebrate with friends and family!

THE NEXT DAY

» Walk for 30 to 60 minutes, very easy. This can be done at one time or in installments.

» Keep drinking about 4 to 6 ounces of water or sports drink like Accelerade every hour.

» Write down what you would do differently in your next race.

15 INSPIRATIONAL STORIES

15.1 BILLY MILLS

The person who inspired me most grew up on the Pine Ridge Native American Reservation in South Dakota. Billy Mills was selected to attend a boarding school where he discovered that he could run faster than other boys in the distance events. Realizing that this could be his path to success in life, he worked very hard and won a scholarship to the University of Kansas.

Billy has a positive sprit and envisioned becoming one of the best distance runners in the NCAA. This did not happen. He came to believe that his best events were longer ones, and he set his sights on the 10,000 meter. His coach, however, wanted him to run shorter events—and lots of them. The training prescribed on the university team did not prepare him for his 10K event, and he did not achieve what he thought was possible during the four years in Lawrence, Kansas.

Post-graduate running programs were few in 1961, but Billy found one: the US Marines. After his officer training he was assigned to the team at Quantico, Virginia, setting his sights on the Olympic 10K. His times were not yet good enough to qualify for the US Olympic Trials, but he felt strongly that he would improve and qualify. Progress was slow.

A college running friend of Billy's returned to his native country of Australia after graduation and trained with the 10K world record holder at the time: Ron Clark. Every week for about three years, Billy would get his "intelligence report," detailing Ron Clark's workouts. Billy tried them but was usually unsuccessful. But at the end of the hard portion of his workout, Billy envisioned that Clark was just ahead of him, so he shifted into his best finish kick and would imagine zooming by the world record holder, breaking the tape and becoming the Olympic champion. Almost every day for three years, this fantasy world was enacted.

In 1963, I went to watch the national cross-country championships in New York City with some college friends. At the meet I looked up an alumnus of my school, Wesleyan University, who was officer in charge of the Marine team. When he discovered that I might be interested in applying in a few years and that I was interested in the 10K, he introduced me to Billy.

I instantly liked Billy. I didn't understand it at the time, but there was something about his attitude that impressed me. Later I came to understand that he had a subtle confidence that I had not encountered before. Billy was probably ranked about 25th going into that race. Without bragging, he told me that he was going to finish near the top. He did.

I followed Billy in *Track & Field News* as he continued to improve, qualified for the Olympic Trials, and then, unexpectedly, made the team in the 10K and the marathon. That experience made a major imprint on me. If Billy could come out of obscurity and make the Olympic Team, maybe there was hope for me.

Billy Mills was not our best 10K runner (Lindgren) and was not ranked very high among the entrants in the 1964 Tokyo Olympics 10K. But somehow he sensed that he had a chance to win. There was no trial heat, only a final with over 60 athletes running 25 times around the track.

The excitement and focus drove Billy to push the pace, and at halfway he realized that he had run only one second slower than his fastest 5K. He was feeling the overexertion and feared that he had spent his resources. He looked for a place to drop out. Just before he stepped off the track, he glanced into the stands and happened to focus on one person: his wife Pat.

He couldn't drop out with her watching, believing in his dream, so he decided to just finish the race. This released the pressure to win. Several runners passed him and then a group of four went by. Something intuitively told Billy that he should go with that group, and he did. Ron Clark was in the group.

Billy admits that he doesn't remember very much about the last four laps. He was running on instinct, trying to put one foot in front of the other, hoping not to fall. The group passed one runner after another, and as they approached the "bell lap" (one to go), Billy was in lane 2, with Ron Clark in lane 1. They were approaching a slower runner who was a full lap behind, and Clark tapped Billy's arm, trying to get him to move out so that both could pass the runner. Billy was so out of it that he didn't know he was being nudged. So Clark finally shoved Billy out into the fourth lane and passed the runner.

The third member of the group, Mohammed Gamudi from Tunisia was right behind, saw the altercation, and took off after Clark. His arms were swinging erratically as he passed Billy, and the sharp part of his elbow hit Billy very hard in his upper arm, hitting a nerve. The pain was great enough to wake Billy up, and the reflex brain sent a primitive message from his playground days: When someone whomps you, you whomp them back. But his slow-twitch endurance muscle cells were spent, and he could not respond. The front two runners moved away from Billy and were about 30 meters ahead as Billy rounded the curve and looked at the finish only 100 meters away.

Billy was living the situation that he had rehearsed almost every day for three years. Without thinking, he did what he had programmed himself to do. And because he had practiced sprinting at the end of his hard workouts, he had trained his fast-twitch muscle fibers to respond.

Billy zoomed by Gamudi and Clark, broke the tape, and became the Olympic champion. This is the greatest come-from-behind victory in the history of the Olympic 10K.

15.2 RACING CANCER

"If I had to choose between my old pre-cancer life as a somewhat depressed, overweight, unmotivated, and unfulfilled couch potato and my current life with cancer, it's easy. I'm energetic, happy, motivated, and love life each day." –*Lee Kilpack*

In 1996 Lee Kilpack was diagnosed with breast cancer, with lymph node involvement. She began a treatment plan of surgery, chemo, and radiation. Lee had never exercised. The diagnosis was a shock to her spirt, and the treatment tested body, mind, and will power.

By 2000, things weren't looking too good, and she felt bad most of the time. Then, one morning she woke up with the desire to start taking care of her body. She hired a personal trainer that day. By 2001, she was walking every day. Later that year she had inserted some running into the walks. In 2002, Lee walked the three-day, 60-mile Breast Cancer Walk and raised $3,000 for the cause.

The training for and the competition of such a strenuous event resulted in a big letdown in motivation, with extended recovery from injuries, aches, and pains. Lee struggled but finally started running regularly in December of 2003. After the 2004 New Year, Lee set a bigger goal—to finish a marathon in November. The training program she chose was too advanced, and she became injured in September. She didn't give up.

In early 2005, her doctor cleared Lee to start running again. She picked up my conservative training program after attending our Blue Mountain Beach retreat. I worked with her via email and often found it hard to hold back her energy and drive.

The training for the Marine Corps Marathon was more of a challenge than most because she relocated to the Gulf coast to volunteer for relief efforts after Hurricane Katrina—squeezing in runs after exhausting days. Somehow, she also hikes, cycles, and paddles hard in her kayak—on the off days, she doesn't run.

She regularly gets screened for tumor markers. While the tests show her out of the normal rage, her doctor does not see a threat in the near future and supports her running.

"I don't know what the future holds for me. If it is metastasis tomorrow, I would be OK with that. What a good life I've been given. My health and happiness have never been better. What my oncologist doesn't understand is what a dynamite combo vitality and endorphins make."

15.3   MARATHON RECORDS AFTER AGE 80

Mavis Lindgren was a sickly child and sickly adult who was advised against exercising. She almost died of a lung infection in her late 50s. During the recovery, her new young doctor had the shocking opinion that she should walk with her husband and kept recommending an increase in the distance she covered.

Surprisingly, Mavis found enjoyment as she felt her body come alive with improved endurance. In her 60s, she took up running with her husband Carl and soon quickly surpassed him. Into her late 80s she was setting age group records and had not even suffered a common cold since beginning her running career.

At about the age of 85 she slipped on a cup at the 20-mile water station at the Portland, Oregon marathon. Officials helped her up and tried to take her to a medical tent. She quietly brushed them off, saying that it was a surface injury. After she finished, however, she went to the medical tent to find that she had been running with a broken arm.

15.4   DAVE WOTTLE: DON'T GIVE UP

Because he was very thin and feeble, the Wottle family doctor recommended exercise, especially running. Dave felt at home on the track team. Like many distance and middle-distance runners, however, he had to work hard to see modest improvements in junior high and high school track. At Bowling Green State University, he improved significantly every year, and Dave moved to the top of the NCAA rankings. He was at his performance peak during the 1972 US Olympic Trials.

While the commentators were expecting running legend Jim Ryun to win the US trials 1500 meters, Dave won easily. He also had no problem winning the 800 meter. During a workout the week after the trials, Dave injured his knee. Three weeks later, when we reported for our Olympic tour, Dave was still injured and had not been able to train.

The coaches wanted to send him home and bring in a healthy runner. Dave refused. Reluctantly the coaches supported him. By working with the athletic trainers and the medical team, he was able to run, and he gradually regained some conditioning.

After the gun fired on his first 800-meter heat in Munich, Dave was at the back of the pack. He struggled to move up as he rounded the final turn, passing one runner, then another. At the finish, he leaned and finished third—the last qualifier for the next round.

Due to conditioning issues, Dave ran a similar race in the next two qualifying heats, coming from behind to barely qualify for the finals.

In the final, the competitors clumped together, going for the gold. Unfortunately, Dave could not keep up and had fallen about 30 yards behind at the halfway mark. Many competitors would have stepped off the track. But Dave set his sights on the next-to-last competitor and caught up with him as they rounded the final curve.

Two runners bumped one another, and Dave darted between them. He ran inside to pass three more and outside to pass another group. As he approached the finish, there was a line of the leaders ahead, and at the last minute a parting occurred, Dave dove through, broke the tape, and won the gold medal.

TV announcers were amazed at his finishing spurt, but this was not the case. His 200-meter splits were almost identical. Dave knew what he could do and stuck with his plan.

At any given point, logic showed that Dave Wottle should have given up his spot and let someone else run. Dave won because he did not give up.

15.5 85 POUNDS LIGHTER— INSPIRED BY A TRAINING GROUP

Tracy B put on the usual weight during her pregnancy and then continued to add more afterward—almost 100 pounds over healthy weight. One day she decided to take small steps, literally, by walking in her neighborhood. Then, she found a charity marathon team that motivated her to take the next step. "The marathon team became a part of me—like a little extension of my family." Instead of restricting her diet, Tracy exercised portion control and eliminated high-fat snacks. Each step reinforced her positive lifestyle as the pounds were burned off during exercise. The best part, according to Tracy, was that she entered a new and wonderful world of exercise.

15.6 LASSE VIREN—WHEN YOU GET KNOCKED DOWN, GET UP

During the Munich Olympics, the star performer in my event, the 10,000, was not well known going into the games. Unlike most athletes who move onto the world class scene over a four- to eight-year period, Lasse's times were not spectacular. When I checked on his performances the year before the Olympics, I noted that he had finished 17th in the European Championships 10K.

Lasse's joy was running through the wilds, mile after mile. He loved forest trails and had a variety of routes and workouts. About the only time that you saw Lasse on a track was during a race. But as Lasse ran his trails, he would envision being in the big race, responding to various challenges and coming back strong.

In the trial heat of the 10,000, Lasse ran a smart race and qualified easily without seeming to be very tired. None of the experts I spoke with before the 10K final predicted that he would finish in the top five.

The 10K final evolved into a strategic race. With about eight laps to go (out of 25), there were 10 runners tightly bunched, all in position to win the race. With no warning, Lasse was tripped by a runner, and he fell into the infield of the track, rolling over.

The first action that impressed me was that Lasse ran straight back to where he had been tripped. If he had tried to run the tangent he would have taken too many steps on the infield and been disqualified. There was no doubt in my mind that he has rehearsed this possibility.

The second impressive action was not trying to catch up with the field in the first lap or two. Lasse gradually caught up with the pack over the next two laps, but he didn't stop there. During the next two laps, he passed one runner at a time.

With two laps to go, Lasse moved into the lead and continued to pick up the pace every 20 yards or so. There were several runners near him with half a lap to go, but Lasse steadily moved away from them. He not only won the Gold, he set a world record.

Lasse won the 5K gold medal in Munich and returned to Montreal four years later to capture the Gold in the 5K and 10K and finish fifth in the marathon.

15.7   145 POUNDS LIGHTER

"I have traded my addiction to food for an addiction to running. I truly believe running has allowed me to cope with the mental and physical stresses of daily life, motherhood, and work more effectively."

Angela was an overweight kid from an obese family. By the age of 35, she weighed 280 pounds with high blood pressure and back, knee, and hip pain. She also had a serious acid reflux problem, and surgery was recommended.

In January of 2005, after months of psychological counseling and exercise (primarily walking and elliptical), she had the gastric bypass operation. She soon discovered that surgery doesn't change a genetic predisposition to obesity, nor the desire to cope with stress by overeating (many patients gain back some of their weight after these surgeries). Because of her surgery, she *had* to eat less and avoid certain foods because of their physical side effects.

Having enjoyed the stress relief of the pre-operation exercise, Angela continued to walk. Six months later and 85 pounds lighter, she decided to step it up by inserting some short running segments into her walks. She then completed a 10K and then a half marathon during the training season. By this time she had lost a total of 120 pounds, crediting running with revving up the fat burning.

Looking for some guidance, she joined our Galloway Training program, finished the Richmond Marathon, and set her sights on the original marathon in Athens, Greece. Despite some health setbacks during the training, she kept improving endurance and lost another 25 pounds. On the difficult Greek course (with a 13-mile hill), Angela set a new personal record by 22 minutes!

15.8   OVERCOMING AN EATING DISORDER

Julie was an overweight child (190 lbs) who enjoyed horseback riding and pop tarts and had self-esteem issues. After breaking her foot from falling off a horse, she fell into depression and didn't eat much for several weeks. For the first time in her life she was receiving a lot of positive attention and let her weight drop to 110!

Calorie intake was so limited that she had no energy to walk or move around at all. Intuitively she felt she needed to run which triggered an appetite increase and a return to a healthy running weight of 145. Then came college. Faced with a lot more activities and stress, she dropped running and used food for comfort. Weight boomed up to over 200 pounds.

Feeling that she could not control her eating habits, Julie engaged in something she could control: running. She felt better about herself, started to lose weight, and trained for a half marathon. Unfortunately she did not take walk breaks and burned out.

Love intervened as Julie and her boyfriend Chris trained for a marathon together. She discovered that the right portion of food, training, and rest intervals gives her the weight and body composition she wants. And she can eat Reese's Peanut Butter Cups—as part of her calorie budget, of course

16 THE MAGIC MILE—
YOUR REALITY CHECK

A major source of stress is setting a goal that is unrealistic. Sadly, many runners don't know what is realistic. In the early 1990s, I started using a one-mile time trial (called a magic mile, or MM) as a reality check on current time goals. After looking at the data from thousands of runners, I've found this to be the best way to predict the best performance possible during a training program. By adding 2 minutes per mile to the predicted marathon pace, you can set a conservative long-run pace that will reduce injury risk. By the end of the training program, I've found the MM to be the best predictor of a potential top performance in an upcoming race.

This one tool gives you control over your goals and your pacing. Making regular "reality checks" on your current potential activates the frontal lobe, taking control over the anxieties that are generated by the reflex brain. Maintaining control and setting realistic goals activate the positive peptides that improve attitude and motivation.

The magic mile (MM) time trials are cognitive checks on your goal. These should be done on the weeks noted on the schedule. The MM has been the best predictor of current potential and helps to set a realistic training pace. With this information, you can decide how hard to run during various situations. (If you have any injuries you should not do the MM.)

» Warm up for the MM with about 10 minutes of very easy running with liberal walk breaks.

» Do four to six accelerations—no sprinting.

» Run around a track if at all possible (or a very accurately measured segment).

» Time yourself for four laps (or an accurately measured mile). Start the watch at the beginning, and keep it running until you cross the finish of the fourth lap.

» On the first MM, don't run all-out, but rather run at a pace that is only slightly faster than your current pace.

» Only one MM is done on each day it is assigned.

» On each successive MM (usually 2-3 weeks later), your mission is to beat the previous best time.

» Don't ever push so hard that you hurt your feet, knees, or any other body part.

» Jog slowly for the rest of the distance assigned on that day, taking as many walk breaks as you wish.

» At the end of the program, do the math listed in the next section, Galloway's Performance Predictor.

» Training pace is at least two minutes per mile slower than predicted maximum marathon pace (MM x 1.3).

After you have run three of these MMs (not at one time; run on different weekends), you'll see progress and will run them hard enough so that you are huffing and puffing during the second half. For prediction purposes, you want to finish feeling like you couldn't go much farther at that pace. Try walking for about 10 to 15 seconds at the half during the MM. Some runners record a faster time when taking short breaks, and some go faster when running continuously. Do what works for you on the MM.

16.1 GALLOWAY'S PERFORMANCE PREDICTOR

Step 1: Run your magic mile time trial (MM) (4 laps around the track).

Step 2: Compute your mile pace for the marathon by multiplying by 1.3

For the half marathon, multiply by 1.2.

For the 10K, multiply by 1.15.

For the 5K, add 33 seconds per mile.

Example:

MM time: 10 minutes

For the best possible marathon pace currently, multiply 10 x 1.3 = 13 min per mile.

For the fastest long-run training pace, add 2 minutes per mile = 15 minutes per mile.

Remember to slow down 30 seconds per mile for every 5 degrees above 60 °F. It's always better to go slower on the long runs.

Current half marathon potential is 12 minutes per mile.

Current 10K potential is 11.5 minutes per mile, or 11:30.

Current 5K potential is 10:33 per mile.

In order to run the time in the race indicated by the MM,

» you have done the training necessary for the goal: long runs, speed sessions, form drills, race rehearsals (see www.jeffgalloway.com);

» you are not injured;

» you run with an even-paced effort;

» the weather on goal race day is not adverse: below 60 °F or 14 °C, no strong head-winds, no heavy rain or snow; and

» there are no crowds to run through or significant hills.

Note: In your first race at any distance, just run to finish. Run the first two thirds of that race at training pace. Then you can choose to continue at that pace or pick it up a bit if you feel good.

16.2 THE LEAP OF FAITH GOAL PREDICTION

I have no problem allowing my e-coach athletes, who've run one or more races at a given distance, to choose a goal time that is faster than that predicted by the MM at the beginning of a six-month program. As you do the speed training, the long runs, and your MMs, you should improve...but how much? In my experience this leap of faith should not exceed 5%. More commonly, the speed-up is in the 3% range.

1. Run the MM time trial.
2. Use the formula presented previously to predict the pace you could run now, if you were in perfect shape for your race.
3. Choose the amount of improvement during the training program (3-5%).
4. Subtract this improvement amount from #2—this is your goal time.

HOW MUCH OF A LEAP OF FAITH?		
Pre-racing season prediction (over a 5- to 6-month training program)	3% improvement	5% improvement
7:00 per mile pace	6:47	6:39
8:00 per mile pace	7:45	7:36
9:00 per mile pace	8:43	8:33
10:00 per mile pace	9:42	9:30
11:00 per mile pace	10:40	10:27
Finish time improvement Pre-season marathon or half prediction	3%	5%
3:00	2:54:36	2:51:00
3:30	2:23:42	3:20:00
4:00	3:52:48	3:48:00

The key to goal setting is keeping your ego in check—and the goal pressure and stress reduced. From my experience, I have found that a 3% improvement is more realistic. This means that if your marathon or half marathon time is predicted to be 3:00, then it is realistic to assume you could lower it by five and a half minutes if you do the speed training and the long runs as noted on my training schedules in this book. The maximum improvement, which is less likely, is a more aggressive 5% or 9 minutes off a three-hour marathon.

In both of these situations, however, everything must come together to produce the predicted result. Even a runner who shoots for a 3% improvement, does all the training as described, achieves his or her goal slightly more than 50% of the time during a racing season. The more aggressive performances usually result in success about 20% of the time. There are many factors that influence your finish time in a race that are outside of your control—weather, terrain, infection, for example. Because of all the variables on race day, it often takes three to four races during a season to achieve success. Don't give up!

16.3 MAGIC MILE TIME TRIALS—COGNITIVE CHECKS THROUGHOUT THE SEASON

» Follow the same format as listed in the pre-test.

» By doing this as noted, you will learn how to pace yourself.

» Hint: It's better to start a bit more slowly than you think you can run.

» Short walk breaks will be helpful for most runners.

» Note whether you are speeding up or slowing down at the end and adjust in the next MM.

» If you are not making progress, then look for reasons and take action.

REASONS WHY YOU MAY NOT BE IMPROVING:

» You've overtrained and are tired—if so, reduce your training for a week and take an extra rest day.

» You may have chosen a goal that is too ambitious for your current ability—set a new goal.

» You may have missed some of your key workouts or too many of your maintenance runs.

» The temperature may have been above 60 °F (14 °C). Higher temperatures will slow you down (the longer the race, the more heat will influence the result).

» You ran the first lap or two too fast.

16.4 FINAL REALITY CHECK

Take the your fastest MM. **If the tests are predicting a time that is slower than the goal you've been training for, go with the time predicted by the magic mile.** It is strongly recommended that you run the first one-third of your goal race a few seconds per mile slower than the pace predicted by the MM average.

16.5 USE A JOURNAL!

Read the next chapter on using a journal. Your odds of reaching your goal increase greatly with this very important instrument. Psychologically, a journal empowers you to take responsibility for the fulfillment of your mission.

17 YOUR JOURNAL—COGNITIVE CONTROL OVER TRAINING

Your running journal can keep you on track while collecting the data you need. Each time you set up your training, record information, or adjust the schedule, you will activate the executive brain. This gives you control over the process and can help you stay away from the emotions generated by the monkey brain.

REGULAR JOURNAL CHECKS CAN REDUCE STRESS

Following a schedule that you believe in will bestow confidence and reduce stress. Regularly seeing the results of your planned workouts energizes your beliefs, builds more confidence, and produces more positive attitude peptides. Your mental interaction with the journal moves you out of the control of the reflex brain and bestows more control over the process.

THIS IS YOUR BOOK

Yes, you are writing a book. You already have the outline: your weekly schedule. As you follow it, your journal will document the good times—and the slow ones. It will allow you to modify your plan and track the changes. Later, you can look back after success or disappointment and often find reasons for either. If we don't look back at the history of our setbacks, we will have a tendency to repeat them.

THE VARIOUS TYPES OF JOURNALS

Calendar—Many runners start recording their runs on a wall calendar—or one that is posted on the refrigerator. Looking at the miles recorded is empowering. But equally motivating for many is the avoidance of too many zeros on days that should have been running days. If you're not sure whether you will really get into this journal process, you may find it easiest to start with a calendar.

A page from my journal

An organized running journal—When you use a product that is designed for running, you don't have to think to record the facts. The spaces on the page ask you for certain info, and you will learn to fill it very quickly. This leaves you time to use some of the open space for the creative thoughts and ideas that pop out during a run. Look at the various journals available and pick one that looks to be easier to use and to carry with you. I've included a sample page of my *Jeff Galloway Training Journal* (available at www.JeffGalloway.com).

Week of _____

Sc = standard course; in = injury; sp = speed; l = long run; sn = scenic; tr = transcendental;
gr = group run; adj = adjustment; fn = fun; fb = fat burning; nu = nutrition
mn = mental training; ag = afterglow; so = social

Monday

Goal		1	Comments
Run/Walk/Run strategy used:		2	
Time:		3	
Distance:		4	
AM Pulse:		5	
Weather:		6	
Temp:		7	
Time:	AM PM	8	
Terrain:		9	
Date Walk Break:		10	

Tuesday

Goal		1	Comments
Run/Walk/Run strategy used:		2	
Time:		3	
Distance:		4	
AM Pulse:		5	
Weather:		6	
Temp:		7	
Time:	AM PM	8	
Terrain:		9	
Date Walk Break:		10	

Wednesday

Goal		1	Comments
Run/Walk/Run strategy used:		2	
Time:		3	
Distance:		4	
AM Pulse:		5	
Weather:		6	
Temp:		7	
Time:	AM PM	8	
Terrain:		9	
Date Walk Break:		10	

Thursday				Comments
	Goal		1	
	Run/Walk/Run strategy used:		2	
	Time:		3	
	Distance:		4	
	AM Pulse:		5	
	Weather:		6	
	Temp:		7	
	Time:	AM PM	8	
	Terrain:		9	
Date	Walk Break:		10	

Friday				Comments
	Goal		1	
	Run/Walk/Run strategy used:		2	
	Time:		3	
	Distance:		4	
	AM Pulse:		5	
	Weather:		6	
	Temp:		7	
	Time:	AM PM	8	
	Terrain:		9	
Date	Walk Break:		10	

Saturday				Comments
	Goal		1	
	Run/Walk/Run strategy used:		2	
	Time:		3	
	Distance:		4	
	AM Pulse:		5	
	Weather:		6	
	Temp:		7	
	Time:	AM PM	8	
	Terrain:		9	
Date	Walk Break:		10	

Sunday				Comments
	Goal		1	
	Run/Walk/Run strategy used:		2	
	Time:		3	
	Distance:		4	
	AM Pulse:		5	
	Weather:		6	
	Temp:		7	
	Time:	AM PM	8	
	Terrain:		9	
Date	Walk Break:		10	

Sample pages of entry from Jeff Galloways Training Journal

Notebook—You don't need to have a commercial product. You can create your own journal by using a basic school notebook of your choice. Find the size that works best with your lifestyle (briefcase, purse, etc.). Following you will find the items that I've found helpful for most runners to record. But the best journals are those that make it easier for you to collect the data you find interesting, while allowing for creativity. The non-limiting nature of a notebook is a more comfortable format for runners who like to write a lot one day, and not so much another day.

Computer logs—There are a growing number of websites and software programs used by runners to record and track their training information. Some electronic devices (mostly GPS) allow you to download data and then sort it. As you set up your own codes and sections, you can manage your training, identify trends, and plan ahead.

THE PLANNING PROCESS—REDUCING STRESS AND ACTIVATING THE CONSCIOUS BRAIN

1. Look over the full training schedule and make any changes needed to customize it for your use.
2. Write down the goal races on the appropriate weeks in your journal. Take a highlighter or other method to make these weeks stand out.
3. Write down the assigned workouts for each day of each week for the next four to eight weeks—in pencil.
4. Look at each of the next eight weeks quickly to make sure you don't have any trips, meetings, or family responsibilities that require adjusting the workouts.
5. Each week, add another week's workouts in pencil and note any changes in your schedule.
6. Each week, look ahead carefully at the next two weeks to ensure that the workouts are adjusted to your real-life schedule.

RECORDING DATA

1. As soon as you can after a run, write the facts in your journal:
    >   Mileage
    >   Pace
    >   Repetitions and times

> Rest interval
> Aches or pains—specifically where and how they hurt
> Problems

In addition, you may also record:

» Time of run
» Total time running
» Weather:
  > Temperature
  > Precipitation
  > Humidity
» Run Walk Run frequency
» Any special segments of the run (speed, hills, race)
» Running companion
» Terrain
» How you felt (scale of 1-10)
» Additional comments

2. Go back over the list again and fill in more details—emotional responses, changes in energy, location of aches and pains—even if they went away during the run. The more information you have, the more likely you are to find patterns that could indicate injury, blood sugar problems, lingering fatigue, as well as why you succeeded in certain races.

3. Helpful additions (usually in a blank section at the bottom of the page) may include:
  > Improvement thoughts
  > Things you should have done differently
  > Interesting happenings
  > Funny things
  > Strange things
  > Stories and right brain crazy thoughts

YOUR MORNING PULSE IS A GREAT GUIDE OF OVERSTRESS

1. Record your morning pulse the moment you wake up. Count your pulse rate for a minute. Record it before you forget it. If you don't have your journal by your bed, then keep a piece of paper and a pen handy.

2. It is natural for there to be some fluctuations based upon the time you wake up and how long you have been awake. But after several weeks and months, these will balance themselves out. The ideal would be to catch the pulse at the instant that you are awake before the shock of an alarm clock or thoughts of work stress.

3. After two weeks or so of readings, you can establish a baseline morning pulse. Remove the top high and low readings and then average the others.

4. The average is your guide. If, on a given day, the rate is 5% higher than your average, take an easy day. When the rate is 10% higher and there is no reason for this (e.g., you woke up from an exciting dream, medication, infection), then your muscles may be tired indeed. Take the day off if you have a run-walk scheduled for that day.

5. If your pulse stays high for more than a week, call your doctor to see if there is a reason for this (e.g., medication, hormones, metabolic changes, infection). This could be due to overtraining.

18 SMOOTH RUNNING FORM REDUCES PAIN AND STRESS

I've heard from hundreds of runners who told me that they had to stop running because of pains in various parts of the body. After doing a running form evaluation, I found one or more problems with their running technique that were often the result of learning poor techniques when young. These bad habits can get hardwired into the reflex brain. When an inefficient range of motion is repeated thousands of times every mile, some aches and pains often occur—producing stress.

But there's hope. When the form is corrected and the right drills are used to reinforce efficient movement, the aggravated area can heal, eliminating or managing the pain. But there's something even more powerful going on. Monitoring running form and making adjustments activates the executive frontal lobe of the brain. The drills in the next chapter allow the conscious brain to retrain the reflex brain to activate efficient and smooth patterns.

SMOOTH RUNNING MEANS USING INERTIA

Your primary mission is to maintain momentum. Very little strength is needed to run—even in shorter races like the 800 meters. During the first hundred meters you'll get your body into the motion and rhythm for your run. After that, the best strategy is to conserve energy while maintaining that forward momentum. To reduce fatigue, aches, and pains, your right brain—helped by muscle memory— intuitively fine-tunes your mechanics and motion to minimize effort.

FORM MISTAKES THAT ADD STRESS AND PRODUCE ACHES AND PAINS

1. Bouncing too much off the ground

2. Using too long of a stride

3. Leaning forward (unless this is natural for the individual)

4. Using an unnatural foot push-off

Humans have many biomechanical adaptations working for them, which have been made more efficient over more than a million years of walking and running. The anatomical running efficiency of the human body originates in the ankle and Achilles tendon—which I treat as a unit. This is no average body part, however, but an extremely sophisticated system of levers, springs, balancing devices, and more. Biomechanics experts believe that this degree of development was not needed for walking. When our ancient ancestors had to run to survive, the ankle and Achilles tendon adapted to endurance running and walking, producing a masterpiece of bioengineering.

Through a series of speed sessions and drills, you can maximize the use of the ankle so that a very little amount of muscle work produces a quicker, consistent forward movement. As you practice these once a week, you'll be able to run farther and faster by using the techniques learned in these drills. Other muscle groups offer support and help to fine-tune the process. When you feel aches and pains that might be due to the way you run, going back to the minimal and gentle use of the ankle and Achilles tendon can often leave you feeling smooth and efficient very quickly.

» **Wobbling**—It all starts with general fatigue that stresses your weak links. For example, if your calf muscles become fatigued at the end of a workout or a race, and you keep pushing to maintain pace, your body will use other muscles and tendons to keep going. You start to wobble because these alternatives are not designed to do the job, stressing the knees, hips, IT band, back, glutes, and hamstrings. The longer you wobble, the more prone you are to injury.

» **Stride extension when tired**—There are several instincts that can hurt us. When tired, for example, many runners extend stride length to maintain pace. This may work for a while—at the expense of the quads, hamstrings, and several other components that become overstressed. It is always better to cut stride and get back into a smooth motion when you feel even a slight aggravation at the end of a run. It's OK to push through tiredness when running smoothly as long as you are not feeling pain in any area. But if this means extending stride or wobbling (which aggravates your weak links), you will pay for this.

» **Be sensitive and avoid irritation**—I don't suggest that everyone try to be a perfect runner. But when you become aware of your form problems and make changes to become more efficient, you'll reprogram the reflex brain to a smoother motion, reducing aches and pains and lowering fatigue. This can also help you run faster.

WHEN UNDER STRESS, USE THE ANKLE

Shorten your stride, keep the feet low to the ground, touch lightly, and the ankle will release in a reflex action, over and over and over. Very little energy is used with this motion. Practice this fast shuffle, and you will program the reflex brain to run this way when needed.

RELAXED MUSCLES ARE IMPORTANT—ESPECIALLY AT THE END OF THE RUN

Overall, the running motion should feel smooth, and there should be no tension in your neck, back, shoulders, or legs. Even during the last half mile of a hard workout or race, try to maintain the three main elements of good form—upright posture, feet low to the ground, and relaxed stride—and you'll stay relaxed. You should not try to push through tightness and pain. Adjust your form to reduce aches and recovery time.

Tip: If you feel yourself tightening up, talk to the muscles, tendons, neck, and back as you make form adjustments. Tell yourself to take a good breath and run like a puppet on a string. This conscious act can help shift control to the conscious frontal brain and away from the reflex brain. As you do the puppet (or whatever helps you relax), you will be reprogramming the reflex brain to do this automatically in the future. It may take dozens of retraining sessions to see this happening.

THREE NEGATIVE STRESSES OF INEFFICIENT FORM

Most runners have an intuitive sense that something is wrong with their form but don't make corrections. The stress builds up and triggers negative attitude secretions:

1. Fatigue from extraneous motions becomes so severe that it takes much longer to recover.

2. Muscles or tendons are pushed beyond capabilities and break down, resulting in pain, injury, or fatigue.

3. The experience is so negative that the desire to run is reduced, producing burnout.

THE BIG THREE: POSTURE, BOUNCE, AND STRIDE

In thousands of individual running form consultations, I've discovered that when runners have problems, they tend to occur in these three running form components: posture, stride, and bounce. Often the problems are like a signature, tending to be very specific to the areas that *you* overuse, because of your unique movement patterns. By making a few small changes in their running forms, most of the runners I've worked with have reduced or eliminated the source of the problems—even the source of pain, when present.

1. POSTURE

Good running posture is actually good body posture. The head is naturally balanced over the shoulders, which are aligned over the hips. As the foot comes underneath, all of these elements are in balance so that no energy is needed to prop up the body. You shouldn't have to work to pull a wayward body back from a wobble or an inefficient motion.

Forward lean—The most common mistake

The posture errors tend to be mostly due to a forward lean—especially when we are tired. The head wants to get to the finish as soon as possible, but the legs can't go any faster. A common tendency at the end of a speed session is to lean with the head. In races, this results in more than a few falls around the finish line. A forward lean will often concentrate fatigue, soreness, and tightness in the lower back or neck. Biomechanics experts note that a forward lean will reduce stride length, causing a slowdown and making running more difficult.

It all starts with the head. When the neck muscles are relaxed, the head can naturally seek an alignment that is balanced on the shoulders. If there is tension in the neck or soreness afterward, the head may lean too far forward. This triggers a more general upper-body imbalance in which the head and chest are suspended slightly ahead of the hips and feet. Sometimes, headaches result from this postural problem. Ask a running companion to tell you if and when your head is too far forward or leaning down. This usually occurs at the end of a tiring run. The ideal position of the head is mostly upright, with the eyes focused about 30 to 40 yards ahead of you. Imagine that you are a puppet on a string.

Sitting back

The hips are the other major postural component that can get out of alignment. When observed from the side, a runner with this problem will have the butt behind the rest of the body. When the pelvic area is shifted back, the legs are not allowed to go through their ideal range of motion, and the stride length is shortened. This produces a slower pace, even when spending significant effort. Many runners tend to hit harder on their heels when their hips are shifted back—but this is not always the case.

A backward lean

It is rare for runners to lean back, but it happens. In my experience, this is usually due to a structural problem in the spine or hips. If you lean backwards, and you're having pain in the neck, back, or hips, you should see an orthopedist that specializes in the back. One symptom is excessive shoe wear on the back of the heel, but there are other reasons why you may show this kind of wear.

Correction—Puppet on a string

The best correction I've found to postural problems has been this mental image exercise: Imagine that you are a puppet on a string. In other words, you're suspended from above—

lifted from the head and each side of the shoulders. In this way, your head lines up above the shoulders, the hips come directly under, and the feet naturally touch lightly directly underneath. It won't hurt anyone to do the puppet several times during a run.

It helps to combine this image with a deep breath. About every four to five minutes, as you start to run after a walk break, exhale more than usual and inhale so that you divert air into the lower lungs. Every third or fourth breath could be a lower lung breath. As you inhale, straighten up and say, "I'm a puppet." Then imagine that you don't have to spend energy maintaining this upright posture, because the "strings" attached from above keep you on track. As you continue to use this visualization, you'll reinforce good posture, and the behavior can be hardwired into your reflex brain.

Upright posture not only allows you to stay relaxed, but you will also probably improve stride length. When you lean forward, you'll be reducing stride to stay balanced. When you straighten up, you'll receive a stride bonus of an inch or so, without any increase in energy. **Note:** Don't try to increase stride length. When it happens naturally, you won't feel it.

An oxygen dividend

Breathing improves when you straighten up. A leaning body can't get ideal use out of the lower lungs. This can cause side pain. When you run upright, the lower lungs can receive adequate air, maximize oxygen absorption, and reduce the chance of side pain.

Note: Over the years, I've found a handful of runners who naturally run with a forward lean. If this is the way you've run and don't have any back, neck, or other problems, continue. Each person should run the way that is natural, and most run upright, according to my experience.

2. BOUNCE

The most efficient stride is a shuffle with feet close to the ground. As long as you pick your foot up enough to avoid stumbling over a rock or uneven pavement, stay low. Most runners don't need to get more than one inch of clearance—even when running fast. As you increase speed and ankle action, you will come off the ground a bit more than this. Again, don't try to increase stride; let this happen naturally.

Your ankle, combined with the Achilles tendon, will act as a spring, moving you forward with each running step. If you stay low to the ground, very little effort is required. Through this shuffling technique, running becomes almost automatic. When runners err on bounce, they try to push off too hard. This usually results in extra effort spent in lifting the body off the ground. You can think of this as energy wasted in the air—energy that could be used to run faster at the end, when it counts.

The other negative force that bouncers experience is that of gravity. The higher you rise, the harder you fall. Each additional bounce off the ground delivers a lot more impact on feet and legs, which during speed sessions, races, and long runs, produces aches, pains, and injuries.

Light touch—Correcting too much bounce

The ideal foot touch should be so light that you don't usually feel yourself pushing off or landing. This means that your foot stays low to the ground and goes through an efficient and natural motion. Instead of trying to overcome gravity, you get in synch with it. If your foot slaps when you run, you will definitely improve with a lighter touch.

Light touch drill

During the middle of a run, time yourself for 20 seconds. Focus on one thing: touching so softly that you don't hear your feet. Earplugs are not allowed for this drill. Imagine that you are running on thin ice or through a bed of hot coals. Do several of these 20-second touches, becoming quieter and quieter with each one. You should feel very little impact on your feet as you do this drill.

3. STRIDE

Studies have shown that as runners get faster, the stride length shortens. This clearly shows that the key to faster and more efficient running is increased cadence or quicker turnover of feet and legs. A major cause of aches, pains, and injuries is a stride length that is too long. When in doubt, it is always better to err on the side of having a shorter stride.

Don't lift your legs.

Even most of the world-class distance runners I've observed over the years don't have a high leg lift. When your legs rise too high, you will overuse the quadriceps muscle (front of the thigh), resulting in a stride that is too long to be efficient. Many runners do this subconsciously at the end of long runs and races. The most common result is sore quadriceps muscles for the next day or two.

Don't kick out too far in front of you.

If you watch the natural movement of the leg, it will kick forward slightly as the running foot gently moves forward, and then land underneath to contact the ground. Let this be a natural motion that leaves no tightness in the muscles behind the lower or upper leg.

Tightness in the front of the shin, behind the knee, or in the hamstring (back of the thigh) are signs that you are kicking too far forward and reaching out too far. Correct this by staying low to the ground, shortening the stride, and lightly touching the ground.

The following drills have helped thousands of runners run more efficiently and faster. Each develops different capabilities, and each rewards the individual for running smoother, reducing impact, using momentum, and increasing the cadence or turnover of feet and legs. With each drill, you'll be teaching yourself to move forward more directly and easily down the road.

These drills should be done on a non-long-run day. It is fine, however, to insert them into your warm-up before a race or a speed workout. Many runners have also told me that both drills are a nice way to break up an average run that otherwise might otherwise be boring.

TROUBLESHOOTING FORM-RELATED INJURIES

Lower back—Caused by forward lean, overstriding, and too few walk breaks

Neck pain—Caused by forward lean and head placed too far forward or back

Hamstring pain—Caused by striding too long and sometimes stretching

Shin pain on front—Caused by too long a stride length, especially on downhills or at the end of a run

Shin pain on inside—Caused by overpronation and uneven terrain

Achilles tendon pain—Caused by stretching, speedwork, and overpronation

Calf pain—Caused by stretching, speedwork, and inadequate number of walk breaks on a long run

Knee pain—Caused by too few walk breaks, overpronation, speedwork, and an extended stride

The shuffle

The most efficient and gentle running form is a shuffle. The feet stay next to the ground, touching lightly with a relatively short stride. When running at the most relaxed range of the shuffling motion, the ankle mechanism does almost all of the work, and little effort is required from the calf muscle.

SPEEDWORK INCREASES RISK FOR INJURY

To improve, time goal runners need to run faster in some workouts, and this means some increase in stride length, greater bounce, and foot push-off. By *gradually* increasing the intensity of speed training, the feet and legs can adapt (with sufficient rest intervals and rest days between). But there is still a risk of injury. Be sensitive to your weak links and don't keep running if there is the chance that you may have the beginnings of an injury. **A gentle increase in the beginning of the season can significantly reduce risk.**

SUGGESTIONS FOR RUNNING SMOOTHER AND REDUCING IRRITATION TO WEAK LINKS:

» Feet should be low to the ground, using a light touch.

» Try not to bounce more than an inch off the ground.

» Let your feet move the way that is natural for them. If you tend to land on your heel and roll forward, do so.

» If you have motion control issues, an orthotic can provide minor correction to bring you into alignment and avoid irritating a weak. A supportive shoe may also be needed. *Check with an experienced podiatrist about these issues.*

» Maintain a gentle stride that allows your leg muscles to stay relaxed. In general, it's better to have a shorter stride, and focus on quicker turnover if you want to speed up.

» Water running can help in eliminating flips and turns of the feet and legs which sometimes cause injuries, aches, or pains. With a flotation device, run in the deep end of the pool so that your foot does not touch the bottom. Even one session of 15 minutes once a week can be beneficial.

19 THE DRILLS

19.1 CADENCE DRILL FOR FASTER TURNOVER

This is an easy drill that helps you to become a smoother runner while also using less effort. As you focus on each of these drills, you activate your conscious brain and gain control over running form improvement. One drill a week will help you step lightly as you increase the number of steps taken per minute. This will help you run faster with greater efficiency.

1. Warm up by walking for 5 minutes and then running and walking very gently for 10 minutes.
2. Start jogging slowly for 1 to 2 minutes, and then time yourself for 30 seconds. During the 30 seconds, count the number of times your left foot touches. Tip: Use a Run Walk Run Timer.
3. Walk around for a minute or so.

4.   On the second 30-second drill, increase the count by 1 or 2.

5.   Repeat this three to seven more times, each time trying to increase by one to two additional steps.

In the process of improving turnover, the human brain takes control and coordinates a series of adaptations which make the feet, legs, nerve system, and timing mechanism work together as an efficient team:

》   Your foot touches more gently.

》   Extra, inefficient motions of the foot and leg are reduced or eliminated.

》   Less effort is spent on pushing up or moving forward.

》   You're lower to the ground—less impact.

》   The ankle becomes more efficient.

》   Aching and pain areas are not overused.

19.2 ACCELERATION-GLIDER DRILLS

Many runners want to run faster but feel awkward and stressed when they try to do so. This is most often due to the lack of gentle training in faster running form. When doing the acceleration-glider regularly, runners find it easier to run faster and smoother. You'll use the conscious brain at the beginning of each of these drills, allowing for training of the reflex brain. Repeat it smoothly four to eight times.

This drill is a very easy and gentle form of speed play, or fartlek. By doing it regularly, you develop a range of speeds, with the muscle conditioning to move smoothly from one to the next. The greatest benefit comes as you learn how to glide or coast off your momentum.

1.   Done on a non-long-run day, in the middle of a shorter run, or as a warm-up for a speed session or a race or MM day.

2.   Warm up with at least half a mile of easy running.

3.   Many runners do the cadence drill just after the easy warm-up, followed by the acceleration-gliders. But each can be done separately, if desired.

4.   Run four to eight of them.

5.   Do this at least once a week.

6.   No sprinting. Never run all-out.

After teaching this drill at my one-day running schools and weekend retreats for years, I can say that most people learn better through practice when they work on the concepts—rather than the details—of the drill. So just get out there and try them!

Gliding—the most important concept. This is like coasting off the momentum of a downhill run. You can do some of your gliders running down a hill if you want, but it is important to do at least two of them on flat terrain.

Do this every week—As in the cadence drills, regularity is very important. If you're like most runners, you won't glide very far at first. Regular practice will help you glide farther and farther.

Don't sweat the small stuff—I've included a general guideline of how many steps to do with each part of the drill, but don't worry about getting any set number of steps. It's best to get into a flow with this drill.

Smooth transition—between each of the components. Each time you shift gears, you are using the momentum of the current mode to start you into the next mode. Don't make a sudden and abrupt change, but have a smooth transition between modes.

Here's how it's done:
Start with a walk of about 10 steps and ease into a shuffle for about 10 steps, smoothly increasing to a slow jog for about 10 steps. Then continue to ease into a regular easy pace for about 10-15 steps. Finally, glide off the momentum seamlessly back into a shuffle and then a walk.

Note: If you are warming up for a MM, race, or speed workout, you could add a 15-20-step gradual acceleration after the regular easy pace segment and then glide back into a shuffle and a walk.

Overall purpose—As you do this drill, every week, your form will become smoother at each mode of running. Congratulations! You are learning how to keep moving at a fairly fast pace without using much energy. This is the main object of the drill.

There will be some drills when you will glide longer than others—don't worry about this. By doing this drill regularly, you will find yourself coasting or gliding down the smallest of inclines, and even for 10 to 20 yards on the flat, on a regular basis. Gliding conserves energy, reduces soreness and fatigue, and helps you maintain a faster pace in races.

20 HILL TRAINING FOR STRENGTH AND RACE PREPARATION

Most of the runners I've coached who are stressed by hills in races have not done much (if any) hill training. As they worry about hills, the negative attitude hormones lower motivation. Running the following workouts at least every 14 days desensitizes runners to the adversity of the hill. Most develop a hill technique that allows them to run on hilly courses without any more fatigue than flat courses. The regular insertion of hill workouts will bestow a significant confidence that helps in every aspect of running and racing, reducing stress and boosting the effect of positive peptides.

Hill training strengthens the legs for running better than any other activity I know. At the same time it can help you maximize an efficient stride length, increase leg speed, and improve your ability to run hills in races. The hill training workouts should not leave you exhausted. Over several weeks, hill work can gently introduce the feet, legs, and cardiovascular system to faster running while also improving confidence.

HILL WORKOUT

» Length:
  › Beginners: 50 to 100 walking steps
  › Intermediate: 100 to 200 walking steps
  › Advanced: 200 to 300 walking steps
» Walk for 2 to 3 minutes.
» Jog and walk to a hill for about 10 minutes. Beginners or runners making a come-back should jog 1 minute and walk 1 minute (a longer warm-up is fine) during the first few weeks of training.
» Do four acceleration-gliders listed in the previous drills section.
» Reverse this warm-up as your cool-down.
» Choose a hill with a moderate grade—steep hills often cause problems.
» Run up the hill for 5 seconds and then down for 5 seconds, gently. Walk for 10 to 15 seconds. Repeat this 5 to 10 times. This finalizes the warm-up.
» Walk for 2 to 3 minutes.
» Run the first few steps of each hill acceleration at a jog, and then gradually pick up the turnover of the feet as you go up the hill.
» Get into a comfortable rhythm so that you can gradually increase this turnover (number of steps per minute) as you go up the hill.
» Keep shortening stride length as you go up the hill.
» It's OK to huff and puff at the top of the hill (due to increased turnover and running uphill), but don't let the legs get overextended or feel exhausted.
» Run over the top of the hill by at least 10 steps.
» Jog back to the top of the hill and walk down to recover between the hills. Walk as much as you need for complete recovery after each hill.

HILL WORKOUT—RUNNING FORM

» Start with a fairly short comfortable stride.
» As you go up the hill, shorten the stride.
» Touch lightly with your feet.
» Maintain a body posture that is perpendicular to the horizontal (upright, not leaning forward or back).

» Pick up the turnover of your feet as you go up and over the top.

» Keep adjusting stride so that the leg muscles don't tighten up—you want them as resilient as possible.

» Relax as you go over the top of the hill, and glide (or coast) a bit on the downside.

HILL TRAINING STRENGTHENS LOWER LEGS AND IMPROVES RUNNING FORM

The incline of the hill forces your legs to work harder as you go up. The extra work up the incline and the faster turnover build strength. By taking an easy walk between the hills and an easy day afterward, the lower leg muscles rebuild stronger. Over several months, the improved strength allows you to support your body weight farther forward on your feet. An extended range of motion of the ankle and Achilles tendon results in a bonus extension of the forward foot—with no increase in effort. You will run faster without working harder. What a deal!

RUNNING FASTER ON HILLS IN RACES

Maintain the same breathing rate as you go up the hill as when on the flat. As you go up the hill, you will shorten the stride. This reduces effort and allows most runners to maintain the same turnover rate of feet as when on flat terrain. Once you train yourself to run with efficient hill form, you'll run faster with increased turnover on the hill workouts. This prepares you to do the same in races. You won't run quite as fast in a race as in your workouts. But through hill training you train yourself to run faster than you used to run up the same hill on a race course.

Hill technique in a race is the same as in workouts: Keep shortening stride as you move up the hill. Monitor your respiration rate; don't huff and puff more than you were doing on the flat. As runners improve their hill technique in races, they find that a shorter and quicker stride reduces effort while increasing speed. The technique is right for the individual when there is no increase in breathing rate even when the turnover rate is increased slightly.

Note: On your long runs and easy running days, just jog up hills. Don't run faster up the hill. If your breathing is increasing on a hill, reduce effort and stride length until your respiration is as it was on the flat ground—or take more frequent walk breaks than when on the flat.

DOWNHILL FORM

» Maintain a light touch of the foot.

» Use an average stride—or quick shuffle.

» Keep feet low to the ground.

» Let gravity pull you down the hill.

» Turnover of the feet will pick up.

» Try to glide (or coast) quickly down the hill.

BIGGEST MISTAKES—TOO LONG A STRIDE AND BOUNCING TOO MUCH

Even when the stride is one or two inches too long, your downhill speed can get out of control. If you are bouncing more than an inch or two off the ground, you'll risk pounding your feet and having to use your quads to slow down (producing soreness) and creating hamstring soreness due to overstriding. Best indicator of overstriding is tight hamstrings and sore quads the next day. Using a quick and slightly shorter stride allows you to run just as fast downhill as with a long stride without sore quads, sore shins, or aggravated hamstrings.

21 THE GALLOWAY
RUN WALK RUN METHOD

The scheduled use of walk breaks bestows mental and physical control over fatigue

By using my method and determining a specific run walk run strategy, you activate the conscious brain. This takes control away from the reflex brain. Your control over this process reduces stress and activates positive attitude hormones. With this method, you choose the length of a run segment. It should be short enough so that you know you can do it. This breaks up the longer runs into segments that are doable. Walk breaks erase fatigue, reduce pain, and lower stress. During the walk break, you can enjoy the endorphin attitude boost.

YOU DETERMINE HOW MUCH YOU RUN AND HOW MUCH YOU WALK

One of the wonderful aspects of running is that there is no definition of a *runner* that you must live up to. There are also no rules that you must follow as you do your daily run. You are the captain of your running ship, and it is you who determines how far, how fast, and how much you run or walk. While you will hear many opinions on this, running has always been a freestyle type of activity in which *each individual is empowered to mix and match the many variables* and come out with the running experience that he or she chooses. Walk breaks can keep the first-time runner away from injury and burnout and can help veterans to improve time. Here's how it works.

WALK BEFORE YOU GET TIRED

Most of us, even when untrained, can walk for several miles before fatigue sets in, because walking is an activity that we are bioengineered to do for hours. Running is more work, because you have to lift your body off the ground and then absorb the shock of the landing, over and over. This is why the continuous use of the running muscles will produce fatigue, aches, and pains much more quickly. If you insert a walk break into a run before your running muscles start to get tired, you allow the muscle to recover instantly, increasing your capacity for exercise while reducing the chance of next-day soreness.

The method part involves having a strategy, which allows the conscious brain to be in command. By using the right ratio of running and walking, you will manage your fatigue. Using this fatigue-reduction tool early will save muscle resources and bestow the mental confidence to cope with any challenges that may come later. Even when you don't need the extra muscle strength and resiliency bestowed by the method, you will feel better during and after your run and finish knowing that you could have gone farther.

Beginners will primarily walk at first. By inserting short segments of running followed by longer walk breaks, your muscles adapt to running without getting overwhelmed. As you improve your running ability, you will reach a point where you can set the ratio of running and walking for that day.

The run-walk method is very simple: You run for a short segment and then take a walk break, and you keep repeating this pattern.

Walk breaks allow you to take control over fatigue in advance so that you can enjoy every run. By taking them early and often, you can feel strong, even after a run that is very long for you. Beginners will alternate very short run segments with short walks. Even elite runners find that walk breaks on long runs allow them to recover faster. There is no need to reach the end of a run feeling exhausted if you insert enough walk breaks, for you, on that day.

WALK BREAKS

» give you control over your fatigue and can virtually eliminate injury;

» give you confidence and stimulate positive attitude hormones;

» erase fatigue for most of the miles on most runs;

» push back your tiredness wall;

» allow for endorphins to collect during each walk break, improving attitude;

» break up the distance into manageable units ("one more minute until a walk break");

» speed recovery;

» reduce the chance of aches, pains, and injury (and the negative peptides they can bring);

» allow you to feel good afterward—doing what you need to do without debilitating fatigue; and

» give you all of the endurance of the distance of each session—without the pain.

A SHORT AND GENTLE WALKING STRIDE

It's better to walk gently with a short stride. There has been some irritation of the shins when runners or walkers maintain a stride that is too long.

NO NEED TO ELIMINATE THE WALK BREAKS

Some beginners assume that they must work toward the day when they don't have to take any walk breaks at all. This is up to the individual, but is not recommended. Remember that you decide what ratio of run walk run to use. There is no rule that requires you to run any ratio of run-walk on any given day. I suggest that you adjust the ratio according to how you feel.

I've run for over 50 years and enjoy running more than ever because of walk breaks. Each run I take energizes my day. I would not be able to run almost every day if I didn't insert the walk breaks early and often. I start most runs taking a short walk break every minute.

HOW TO KEEP TRACK OF THE WALK BREAKS

There is now a Galloway timer that beeps and vibrates (about $20). There are also several watches that can be set to beep when it's time to walk and then beep again when it's time to start up again. Check my website *www.jeffgalloway.com* or a good running store for advice in this area.

HOW TO USE WALK BREAKS

1. Beginners usually start by running for 5 to 10 seconds, walking for the rest of each minute.
2. Veterans can use the following guide, based upon pace per mile, to set up the walk breaks. If you feel good during and after the run, continue with this ratio. If not, run less until you feel good.
3. When challenged, decrease the run amount and increase the walk.
4. On long runs, take the walk breaks a lot more frequently to speed up recovery.
5. Veterans can reduce or eliminate walk breaks during the last 25% of their races.

WALK BREAK STRATEGIES

The frequency of walk breaks is usually tied to the pace per mile. But it is always OK to walk more frequently if you want or need to do so. Here are the current strategies:

RUN WALK RUN STRATEGIES

Pace per mile	Run time/Walk time
7:00	6 minutes/30 seconds (or run a mile/walk 40 seconds
7:30	5 minutes/30 seconds
8:00	4 minutes/30 seconds (or 2 minutes/15 seconds)
8:30	3 minutes/30 seconds (or 2 minutes/20 seconds)
9:00	2 minutes/30 seconds (or 80 seconds/20 seconds)
9:30 – 10:45	90 seconds/30 seconds (or 60/20, 45/15, 60/30, or 40/20)
10:45 – 12:15	60 seconds/30 seconds (or 40/20, 30/15, 30/30, or 20/20)
12:15 – 14:30	30 seconds/30 seconds (or 20/20 or 15/15)
14:30 – 15:45	15 seconds/30 seconds
15:45 – 17:00	10 seconds/30 seconds
17:00 – 18:30	8 seconds/30 seconds (or 5/25 or 10/30)
18:30 – 20:00	5 seconds/30 seconds (or 5/25 or 4/30)

Note: You may always divide each of the amounts by 2. Example: Instead of running a 9 minutes per mile pace using 2 minutes run/30 seconds walk, you could run for 60 seconds and walk for 15 seconds.

22 COGNITIVE FOCUS ON ADEQUATE BLOOD SUGAR = MOTIVATION

Your blood sugar level (BSL) determines how good you feel, and a low level is a source of stress. Blood glucose is your brain's only fuel, and the brain monitors this carefully. When the level gets even a bit too low, negative hormones increase, lowering motivation. When BSL is adequate, the receptor cells receive good messages, and positive attitude hormones transmit positive messages throughout the mind–body network. If you eat too much sugar, starch, or other simple carbohydrate, your BSL can rise too high. You'll feel really good for a while. But the excess sugar triggers a release of insulin, which can push BSL too low. In this state, your reflex brain is under stress and reduces blood flow to the frontal lobe, resulting in foggy thinking. If the BSL is not raised, negative peptides are produced, lowering motivation and energy level.

When BSL is maintained at a stable level throughout the day, you will be more motivated to do most activities, including exercise. You'll have a more positive mental attitude and will be more likely to deal with stress and problem solving. Just as eating at regular intervals throughout the day maintains metabolism, the steady infusion of balanced nutrients all day long will maintain stable blood sugar levels, sending positive peptide messages between the body and mind that everything is OK.

See my books *Women's Complete Guide to Running, Running and Fat Burning for Women,* or *Nutrition for Runners* for more meal planning information.

If your BSL is low, the simple act of eating a snack containing 80% simple carbohydrate and about 20% protein 30 minutes or less before your workout will boost the BSL and stimulate positive peptides, improving attitude and helping you to get out the door.

EAT EVERY TWO TO THREE HOURS

When exercisers experiment with various snacks, most find that an individualized arrangement of small meals produces a more stable BSL.

DO I HAVE TO EAT BEFORE A WORKOUT?

Only if the BSL is low. Most who exercise in the morning don't need to eat anything before the start. As mentioned, if your blood sugar level is low in the afternoon and you have a workout scheduled, a BSL snack can help. If you feel that a morning snack will help, the only issue is to avoid consuming so much that you get an upset stomach.

For best results in raising blood sugar levels when they are too low (within 30 minutes before exercise), try different snacks. The product Accelerade has worked best among the thousands of exercisers I hear from every year. It has the 80%:20% ratio of carb to protein. If you eat an energy bar with the 80:20 ratio, be sure to drink 6 to 8 ounces of water at the same time.

EATING DURING EXERCISE

Most exercisers don't need to worry about eating or drinking during a run or walk until the length of the session exceeds 60 minutes (for most of my clients, 90 minutes). At this point, there are several options.

» On runs longer than an hour, many runners like to use a BSL booster. Practice various eating strategies on your long run-walks and pick what works best.

» Rule of thumb: 30 to 40 calories every 2 miles.

» Gel products—These come in small packets and are the consistency of honey or thick syrup. The most successful way to take them is to put one to two packets into a small plastic bottle with a pop-top. About every 10 to 15 minutes, take a squirt or two, with a sip or two of water.

» Energy bars—Cut a bar into 8 to 10 pieces and take a piece with a couple of sips of water every 10 to 15 minutes

» Candy/sugar—When consumed during exercise, sugary snacks have produced the quickest boosting effect among the runners I've monitored. The usual consumption is 30 to 40 calories about every 10 to 15 minutes

» Sports drinks—Since there is significant percentage of nausea episodes among those who drink these during exercise, this is not my top recommendation. If you have found that a product works for you, use it exactly as you have used it before.

RELOAD WITHIN 30 MINUTES AFTER EXERCISE

Whenever you have finished a hard or long workout (for you), a reloading snack of 100 to 300 calories will help you recover faster. Products with 80% simple carbs and 20% protein have been shown to be most successful in reloading the muscles. The product that has worked best among the thousands I work with each year is Endurox R4.

23 TROUBLESHOOTING

Knowing that there is a solution keeps you in the human brain, reduces stress, and improves attitude

» How do I start back when I've had time off?

» It hurts! Is it just a passing ache or real injury?

» No energy today

» Side pain

» I feel great one day, but the next day...

» Cramps in my leg muscles

» Upset stomach or diarrhea

» Headache

» Should I run when I have a cold?

» Street safety

» Dogs

HOW DO I START BACK WHEN I'VE HAD TIME OFF?

Many runners who take time off from running feel stressed when they start back. When the stress is high, the reflex brain triggers a series of actions that reduce motivation, including reduction of blood flow to key muscles, the brain, and the gut. It will also trigger negative attitude hormones that reduce motivation further. The longer you've been away from running, the greater the benefit from a plan which will allow the conscious brain to assume control over the anxiety-ridden reflex brain.

The use of walk breaks greatly improves confidence and attitude. Success is increased when you believe in your plan, and take conscious involvement to get out the door (review the chapter that details how to handle certain situations). I want to warn you now that you will reach a point when you feel totally back in shape—but you are not. Stay with the following plan for your return, and when in doubt, be more conservative. Remember that you are in this for the long run!

Note: I suggest using the proven training schedules in my books *Marathon: You Can Do It, Running: A Year Round Plan, Galloway Training Programs, 5K/10K Running, Half-Marathon: You Can Do It, Cross-Country Running, or Running: Testing Yourself*. Each week's workouts are numbered in sequence, leading to the goal.

Less than 2 weeks off—You will feel like you are starting over again, but you should come back quickly. Look at the schedules. Let's say that you were at week 20 but had to take 10 days off. Start back at week 2 for the first week. If all is well, skip to week 10 or 11 for the second week. If that works well, ease into week 17 or 18, and then move back into week 20.

14 to 29 days off—You will also feel like you are starting over again, and it will take longer to get it all back. Within about five to six weeks, you should be back to normal. Use the schedule of your choice (from week 1) for two weeks. If there are no aches, pains, or lingering fatigue, then use the schedule but skip every other week. After the fifth week, transition back into what you were doing before the layoff.

One month or more off—If you have not run for a month or more, start over again like a beginner. Use one of the schedules, following it exactly (from week 1) for the first few weeks. After two to three weeks, the safest plan is to continue with the schedule. But if you don't have aches, pains, or lingering fatigue, you could increase more rapidly by skipping one week out of three. After two months of no problems, your conditioning should have returned.

IT HURTS! IS IT JUST A PASSING ACHE OR A REAL INJURY?

The one downside to effective mental training is that you can keep running when you have an injury and make it worse. So it is important to know whether it is TMS or just an ache or pain that is part of the training process.

Most of the aches and pains felt when running are temporary body adjustments. They don't indicate a serious problem and will go away within a few minutes—or at least within 36 hours. Research shows that runners over the age of 50 have fewer orthopedic problems compared with non-runners the same age. But if you try to run when there is a potential injury, you can make the ache worse, requiring more time for recovery.

If the pain comes on when running, just walk for an additional 2 minutes, jog a few strides, and walk another 2 minutes. If it still hurts after doing this four or five times, stop running and walk. If the pain goes away when you walk, just walk for the rest of the workout.

Walking pain—When the pain stays around when walking, use a very short stride. Walk slowly for 30 to 60 seconds. If it still hurts when walking, sit down and massage the area that hurts, if you can. Sit for two to four minutes. When you try again to walk, and it still hurts, call it a day—your workout is over.

It's an injury if...

Inflammation—There is swelling in the area.

Loss of function—The foot or knee, for example, doesn't work correctly.

Pain—It hurts and keeps hurting or gets worse.

TREATMENT SUGGESTIONS:

1. See a doctor who has treated other runners very successfully and wants to get you back on the road or trail.
2. Take at least two to five days off from any activity that could irritate it to get the healing started—take more if needed.
3. If the area is next to the skin, rub a chunk of ice on the area, constantly rubbing for 15 minutes until the area gets numb. Continue to do this for a week after you feel no symptoms. Ice bags and gel ice do virtually no good at all according to my experience.

4.   If the problem is inside a joint or muscle, call your doctor and ask if you can use prescription strength anti-inflammatory medication. Don't take any medication without a doctor's advice—and follow that advice.

5.   If you have a muscle injury, see a veteran sports massage therapist. Try to find one who has a lot of successful experience treating the area where you are injured. The magic fingers and hands can often work wonders.

6.   Read the section on TMS. A high percentage of runner's aches and pains come from TMS which can be dealt with. See the TMS section in this book, page_____.

7.   Belief in treatment mode can energize your organism for healing and increase positive peptides.

This is advice from one runner to another. For more info on injuries and treatment, see a doctor and read *Running Injuries: Treatment and Prevention* by Hannaford and Galloway.

NO ENERGY TODAY

There will be a number of days each year when you will not feel like exercising. On most of these, you can turn it around and feel great. Occasionally, you will not be able to do this, because of an infection, lingering fatigue, or other physical problems. Here's a list of things that can give you energy. If these actions don't lead you to a run, then read the nutrition sections—particularly the previous chapter on blood sugar levels—in *Running and Fat Burning for Women or Nutrition for Runners*.

1.   Eat an energy bar with water or caffeinated beverage about an hour before the run. Caffeine helps!

2.   Instead of the first option, 30 minutes before exercising, you could drink 100 to 200 calories of a sports drink that has a mix of 80% simple carbohydrate and 20% protein. The product Accelerade already has this ratio.

3.   Just walk for 5 minutes away from your house or office, and the energy often kicks in. Forward movement gets the attitude moving, too.

4.   One of the prime reasons for no energy is not reloading within 30 minutes after your last exercise session. Consume 200 to 300 calories of a mix that is 80% simple carbohydrate and 20% protein (Endurox R4 is the product that has this formulation).

5.   Low-carb diets will result in low energy, low blood sugar level, and low motivation before and during a workout.

6. In most cases it is fine to keep going even if you aren't energetic. But if you sense an infection, see a doctor. If the low energy stays around for several weeks, see a nutritionist who knows about the special needs of runners or get some blood work done. This may be due to inadequate iron, B vitamins, protein, or energy stores.

Note: If you have any problems with caffeine, don't consume any products containing it. As always, if you sense any health problem, see a doctor.

SIDE PAIN

This is very common and usually has a simple fix. Normally you should not worry about this—it just hurts. This condition is due to 1) the lack of lower lung breathing and 2) going a little too fast from the beginning of the run. You can correct number 2 easily by walking more at the beginning and slowing down your running pace for the first 10 minutes of the run.

Lower lung breathing from the beginning of a run can prevent side pain. This way of inhaling air is performed by diverting the air you breathe into your lower lungs. Also called *belly breathing,* this is how we breathe when asleep, and it provides maximum opportunity for oxygen absorption. If you don't breathe this way from the start of the run and you are not getting the oxygen you need, the side pain will tell you. By slowing down, walking, and breathing deeply for a while, the pain may go away. But sometimes it does not. Most runners just continue to run and walk with the side pain. In 50 years of running and helping others run, I've not seen any lasting negative effect from those who run with a side pain. But you can prevent this by breathing properly.

A maximum breath is not needed. Simply breathe a normal breath but send it to the lower lungs. You know that you have done this if your stomach goes up and down as you inhale and exhale. If your upper chest goes up and down, you are not bringing a lot of air into the lower lungs.

Note: Never breathe in and out rapidly. This can lead to hyperventilation, dizziness, and fainting.

I FEEL GREAT ONE DAY, BUT THE NEXT DAY...

If you can solve this problem, you could become a very wealthy person. There are a few common reasons for this, but there will always be "those days" when the body doesn't seem to work right, the gravity seems heavier than normal, and you cannot find a reason.

1. **Push through**—In most cases, this is a one-day occurrence. Most runners just put more walking into the mix and get through it. Before pushing, however, make sure that you don't have a medical reason why you feel bad. Don't exercise when you have a lung infection, for example.

2. **Heat and humidity will make you feel worse**—You will often feel great when the temperature is below 60 ˚F and miserable when 80 ˚F or above (especially at the end of the workout). During hot periods, try to exercise before the sun gets above the horizon.

3. **Low blood sugar can make any run a bad run**—You may feel good at the start but suddenly feel like you have no energy. Every step seems to take a major effort. Read the previous chapter on blood sugar levels.

4. **Low motivation**—Use the rehearsal techniques in chapter on situations to get you out the door on a bad day. These have helped numerous runners turn their minds around—even in the middle of a run.

5. **Infections**—Infection can leave you feeling lethargic, achy, and unable to run at the same pace that was easy a few days earlier. Check the normal signs (fever, chills, swollen lymph glands) and at least call your doctor if you suspect something.

6. **Medication and alcohol,** even when taken the day before, can leave a hangover that dampens a workout.

7. **A slower start** can make the difference between a good day and a bad day. When your body is on the edge of fatigue or other stress, it only takes a few seconds too fast per mile, walking or running, to push into discomfort or worse.

CRAMPS IN MY MUSCLES

At some point, most runners experience cramps. These muscle contractions usually occur in the feet or the calf muscles and may come during a run or walk, or they may hit at random. Most commonly, they will occur at night or when you are sitting around at your desk or watching TV in the afternoon or evening.

If you are dehydrated at the start of your run, you are more likely to experience cramps. Avoid alcohol and salty foods and hydrate well the day before a long run. A good sports drink like Accelerade, taken throughout the day before, will help to keep your fluid levels and your electrolytes topped off (maximum of 16 oz. per day).

If you have had several cramping episodes or one severe experience, the reflex brain remembers. For several weeks afterward, the reflex brain will trigger negative attitude peptides when you think about running. It is also possible that the reflex brain has reduced blood flow to the muscles, in response to the stress. See the chapter on situations for ways of getting back into the flow of running.

Cramps vary in severity. Most are mild, but some can grab so hard that they shut down the muscles and hurt when they seize up. Massage and a short, gentle movement of the muscle can help to bring most of the cramps around. Odds are that stretching will make the cramp worse or tear the muscle fibers. There may be soreness in the cramped muscles for several days. On the short running days, take a longer walk as warm-up and adjust the run walk run ratio to include more walking.

Most cramps are due to overuse, exercising farther or faster than in the recent past, or continuing to put yourself at your limit, especially in warm weather. Look at the pace and distance of your runs and run walk run strategy in your training journal to see if you have been running too far, or too fast, or have not taken walk breaks liberally enough.

» Continuous running increases cramping. Taking walk breaks more often can reduce or eliminate cramps. Many runners who used to cramp when they ran one minute and walked one minute stopped cramping with a ratio of run 30 seconds and walk 30 to 60 seconds.

» When a cramp has occurred, it may be necessary to take a shuffle break instead of a walk break. Shuffling is a minimal running motion in which the ankle is providing most of the energy and propulsion: short stride, feet next to the ground, light touch.

» Prolonged dehydration. Drink eight 7-ounce glasses of water a day plus one or two glasses of either electrolyte beverage or orange juice. During hot weather, a good electrolyte beverage can help to replace the salts that your body loses in sweating. A drink like Accelerade, for example, can help to top off these minerals after a very long run. Drink approximately 6 to 8 ounces every one to two hours.

» On very long hikes, walks, or runs, however, the continuous sweating, especially when drinking a lot of fluid, can push your sodium levels too low and produce muscle cramping. If this happens regularly, a buffered salt tablet has helped greatly. SUCCEED is used by many runners in ultramarathons and Ironman events.

» Many medications, especially those designed to lower cholesterol, have muscle cramps as one of their known side effects. Runners who use medications and experience muscle cramps should ask their doctor if there are alternatives.

HERE ARE SEVERAL WAYS OF DEALING WITH CRAMPS:

1. Take a longer and more gentle warm-up.
2. When you start running, go slower.
3. Shorten your run segment.
4. Slow down your walk, and walk more.
5. Shorten your distance on a hot and humid day.
6. Break your run up into two segments.
7. Look at any other exercise that could be causing the cramps.
8. Take a buffered salt tablet at the beginning of your exercise.
9. Shorten your stride—especially on hills.

Note: If you have high blood pressure, ask your doctor before taking any salt product.

UPSET STOMACH OR DIARRHEA

Nausea and diarrhea (N/D) are triggered by stress. Most commonly, it is the stress of running on that day due to the causes listed here. But stress can come from many unique conditions within the individual. Your reflex brain triggers the N/D to get you to reduce the exercise, which will reduce at least one source of stress. Here are the common causes.

1. **Running too fast or too far**—This is the most common cause. Runners are confused about this, because the pace doesn't feel too fast in the beginning. Each person has a level of fatigue that triggers these conditions. Slowing down and taking more walk breaks from the beginning will help you manage the problem.

2. **Eating too much or too soon before the run**—Your system has to work hard when you're running, and it works hard to digest food. Doing both at the same time raises stress and results in nausea. Having food in your stomach in the process of being digested is an extra stress and a likely target for elimination.

3. **Eating a high-fat or high-protein diet**—Even one meal that has over 50% of the calories in fat or protein can lead to N/D one to four hours later if you are running.

4. **Eating too much the afternoon or evening on the day before**—A big evening meal will still be in the gut the next morning, being digested. When you bounce up and down on a run, which you will, you add stress to the system often producing N/D.

5. **Heat and humidity**—These are a major cause of these problems. Some people don't adapt to heat well and experience N/D with minimal build-up of temperature or humidity. But in hot conditions, everyone has a core body temperature increase that will result in significant stress to the system—often causing nausea and sometimes diarrhea. By slowing down, taking more walk breaks, and pouring water over your head, you can manage this better. The best time to exercise in warm weather is before the sun gets above the horizon.

6. **Drinking too much water *before* a run**—If you have too much water in your stomach and you are bouncing around, you increase stress on the digestive system. Reduce your intake to the bare minimum (one 4- to 6-oz portion, right after getting out of bed). Most runners don't need to drink any fluid before a run that is 60 minutes or less.

7. **Drinking too much of a sugar or electrolyte drink**—Water is the easiest substance for the body to process. The addition of sugar or electrolyte minerals, such as in a sports drink, makes the substance harder to digest for many runners. During a run (especially on a hot day), it is best to drink only water. Cold water is best.

8. **Drinking too much fluid too soon after a run**—Even if you are very thirsty, don't gulp down large quantities of any fluid. Try to drink no more than 6 to 7 ounces every 20 minutes or so. If you are particularly prone to this N/D, just take two to four sips every five minutes or so. When the body is very stressed and tired, it's not a good idea to consume a sugar drink. The extra stress of digesting the sugar can lead to problems.

9. **Don't let running be stressful to you**—Some runners get too obsessed about inserting a run into every single day or running at a specific pace. This adds stress to your life. Relax and let your run diffuse some of the other tensions in your life.

HEADACHE

There are several reasons why runners get headaches on runs. While uncommon, they happen to the average runner about one to five times a year. The extra stress that running puts on the body can trigger a TMS headache on a tough day—even with the relaxation that comes from the run. Many runners find that a dose of an over-the-counter headache medication takes care of the problem. As always, consult with your doctor about use of medication. Here are some major causes and solutions.

Dehydration—If you run in the morning, make sure that you hydrate well the day before. Avoid alcohol if you run in the mornings and have headaches. Also watch the salt in your dinner meal the night before. A good sports drink like Accelerade taken throughout the day before will help to keep your fluid levels and your electrolytes topped off (maximum of 16 oz. per day). If you run in the afternoon, follow the same advice leading up to your run on the day of the run.

Medications can often produce dehydration—There are some medications that make runners more prone to headaches. Check with your doctor.

Too hot for you—Run at a cooler time of the day (usually in the morning before the sun gets above the horizon). When on a hot run, pour water over your head. Take more frequent walk breaks.

Running a little too fast—Start all runs more slowly, and walk more during the first half of the run.

Running farther than you have run in the recent past—Monitor your mileage, and don't increase more than about 15% farther than you have run on any single run in the past week.

Low blood sugar level—Be sure to boost your BLS with a snack about 30 to 60 minutes before you run. If you are used to having it, caffeine in a beverage can sometimes help this situation also.

Prone to migraines—There are many individual issues here. Try your best to avoid dehydration. Talk to your doctor about other possibilities. Read the section on TMS.

Watch your neck and lower back—If you have a slight forward lean as you run, you can put pressure on the spine, particularly in the neck and lower back. Read the chapter, Smooth Running Form Reduces Pain and Stress. Be a puppet on a string.

SHOULD I RUN WHEN I HAVE A COLD?

Talk to your doctor when you have an infection. There are many individual health issues. Usually you will be given the OK to gently exercise.

Lung infection—Don't run! A virus in the lungs can move into the heart and kill you. Lung infections are usually indicated by coughing.

Common cold—There are many infections that initially seem to be a normal cold but are not. At least call your doctor's office to get clearance before running. Be sure to explain how much you are running, and what, if any, medication you are taking.

Throat and sinus infection—Most runners will be given the OK, but check with the doctor.

STREET SAFETY

Each year several runners are hit by cars when running. Most of these are preventable. Here are the primary reasons and what you can do about them.

1. **The driver is intoxicated or preoccupied by cellphone**—Always be on guard, even when running on the sidewalk or pedestrian trail. Many of the fatal crashes occurred when the driver lost control of the car and came up behind the runner on the wrong side of the road. I know it is wonderful to be on cruise control in your right brain,

but you can avoid a life-threatening situation if you will just keep looking around and anticipating. Wear a blinking light or reflective gear after dark. I recommend the NiteBeams products.

2. **The runner dashes across an intersection against the traffic light**—When running or walking with another person, don't try to follow blindly across an intersection. Runners who quickly sprint across the street without looking are often surprised by cars coming from unexpected directions. The best rule is the one that you heard as a child: When you get to an intersection, stop, look both ways, and look both ways again (and again) before crossing. Have an option to bail out of the crossing if a car surprises you from any direction.

3. **Runners wander out into the street as they talk and run**—One of the very positive aspects of running becomes a negative one in this case. Yes, chat and enjoy time with your friends. But every runner in a group needs to be responsible for his or her own safety, footing. Runners at the back of a group mistakenly assume that they don't have to be concerned about traffic at all. This results in a very risky situation.

In general, be ready to save yourself from a variety of traffic problems by following these rules and any others that apply to specific situations. Even though the rules below seem obvious, many runners who are hit by cars tend to ignore them.

» Be constantly aware of vehicular traffic at all times.

» Assume that all drivers are drunk, crazy, or both. When you see a strange movement by a car, be ready to get out of the way.

» Mentally practice running for safety. Get into the practice of thinking ahead at all times with a plan for that current stretch of road.

» Run as far off the road as you can. If possible, run on a sidewalk or pedestrian trail.

» Run facing traffic. A high percentage of traffic deaths come from those who run with the flow of traffic and do not see the threat from behind.

» Wear lights or reflective gear at night. NiteBeams have several products that blink and provide great protection.

» Take control over your safety—you are the only person who can best protect yourself

23.1   DOGS

When you enter a dog's territory, you may be in for a confrontation. Here are my suggestions for dealing with your "dog days:"

» There are several good devices that will help deter dogs: a stick, rocks, some electronic signal devices, and pepper spray. If you are in a new area or an area of known dogs, I recommend that you have one of these at all times.

» At the first sign of a dog ahead or barking, try to figure out where the dog is located, whether the dog is a real threat, and what territory the dog is guarding.

» The best option is to run a different route.

» If you really want or need to run past the dog, pick up a rock if you don't have another anti-dog device.

» Watch the tail. If the tail does not wag, beware.

» As you approach the dog, it is natural for the dog to bark and head toward you. Raise your rock as if you will throw it at the dog. In my experience, the dog withdraws about 90% of the time. You may need to do this several times before getting through the dog's territory. Keep your arms up.

» In a few cases you will need to throw the rock and sometimes another if the dog keeps coming.

» In less than 1% of the hundreds of dog confrontations I've had, there is something wrong with the dog, and it continues to move toward you. Usually the hair will be up on the dog's back. Try to find a barrier to get behind and, yell loudly in hopes that the owner or someone will help you. If a car comes by, try to flag down the driver and either stay behind the car as you get out of the dog's territory or get in the car for protection if that is appropriate.

» Develop your own voice. Some use a deep commanding voice, and some use a high-pitched voice. Whichever you use, exude confidence and command.

24 INJURY TROUBLESHOOTING

For more information, see *Running Injuries: Treatment and Prevention* by Hannaford and Galloway, available at www.JeffGalloway.com

QUICK TREATMENT TIPS

For all injuries:

» Read the section on TMS on page 82.

» Take three days off from running or any activity that could aggravate the area.

» Avoid any activity that could aggravate the injury.

» As you return to running, stay below the threshold of further irritation with much more liberal walking.

» Don't stretch. Stretching keeps most injuries from healing. Iliotibial stretches, however, can sometimes allow for running when the IT band tightens up.

Muscle injuries:

» Call your doctor's office and see if you can take prescription strength anti-inflammatory medication.

» See a sports massage therapist who has worked successfully on many runners.

Tendon and foot injuries:

» Rub a chunk of ice directly on the area for 15 minutes every night (keep rubbing until the area gets numb—about 15 minutes). **Note:** ice bags, or gel ice don't seem to help in my experience.

» Foot injuries sometimes are helped by a boot cast at first to let the problem start healing.

Knee injuries:

» Call your doctor's office to see if you can take prescription-strength anti-inflammatory medication.

» See if you can do a little gentle walking as sometimes this helps.

» Sometimes the knee straps can relieve pain; ask your doctor.

» Get a shoe check to see if you are in the right shoe.

» If you overpronate, an orthotic or motion-control shoe may help.

» If you have internal knee pain, a glucosamine supplement may help.

» If you have IT band injury, using a foam roller has helped. Roll for five minutes before bed, and, if possible, five minutes before and after a run.

Shin injuries:

» Rule out a stress fracture. In this case, the pain usually gets worse as you run, but check with your doctor. If it is a stress fracture, you must stop running for (usually) at least eight weeks.

» If the pain gradually goes away as you run on it, there is less worry of a stress fracture. This is probably a shin splint. If you stay below the threshold of irritating the shin muscle, you can run with shin splints as they gradually go away (check with doctor to be sure).

» Take more walk breaks and run more slowly.

Starting running before the injury has healed

With most running injuries, you can continue to run even while the injury is healing. But first, you must have some time off to get the healing started. If you do this at the beginning of an injury, you will usually only need two to five days off. The longer you try to push through the problem, the more damage you produce, and the longer it will take to heal. Stay in touch with the doctor at any stage of this healing–running process, follow his or her advice, and use your best judgement.

To allow for healing, once you have returned to running, stay below the threshold of further irritation. In other words, if the injury feels a little irritated when running at 2.5 miles and starts hurting a little at 3 miles, you should run no more than 2 miles. And if your run-walk ratio is 3 minutes run/1 minute walk, you should drop back to 1/1, or 30 seconds/30 seconds.

Take a day of rest between running days. With most injuries, you can crosstrain to maintain conditioning, but make sure that your injury will allow this. Again, your doctor can advise.

Best crosstraining modes to maintain your running conditioning
Before doing any of these, talk to your doctor. Most are fine for most injuries, but some run a risk of irritating the injured area and delaying the healing process. For more information on this, see the chapter on crosstraining in *Galloway's Book on Running, Second Edition*. Gradually build up the crosstraining, because you have to condition those muscles gradually, too. Even walking is a great way to maintain conditioning if the injury and the doctor will allow it.

» Running in the water to improve your running form
» NordicTrack machines
» Walking
» Rowing machines
» Elliptical machines

See a doctor for medical issues.

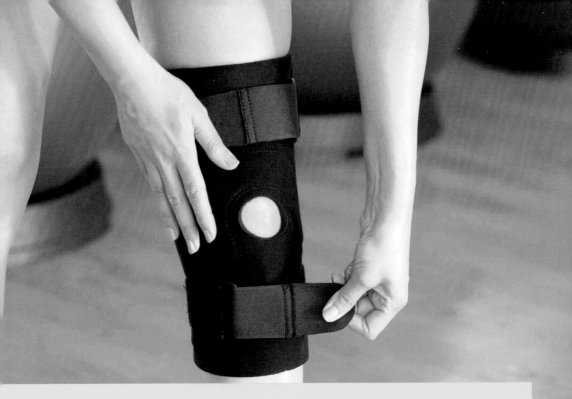

25 TREATMENT SUGGESTIONS FROM ONE RUNNER TO ANOTHER

Taking some action to get the healing started and then treating it will build confidence, produce positive attitude peptides, and mobilize your body, mind, and spirit for healing. Believing in the treatment will also help.

Note: For more information, see *Running Injuries: Treatment and Prevention* by Hannaford and Galloway, available at *www.JeffGalloway.com*.

KNEE PAIN

Most knee problems will go away if you take five days off. Ask your doctor if you can use anti-inflammatory medication. Try to figure out what caused the knee problem. Make sure that your running courses don't have a slant or canter. Look at the most worn pair of shoes you have, even walking shoes. If there is wear on the inside of the forefoot, you probably overpronate. If you have repeat issues with knee pain, you may need a foot support or orthotic. If there is pain under the kneecap or arthritis, glucosamine/chondroitin products may help. The best I've found in this category is Joint Maintenance Product by Cooper Complete.

PAIN OUTSIDE OF THE KNEE—ILIOTIBIAL BAND SYNDROME

This band of fascia acts as a tendon going down the outside of the leg from the hip to just below the knee. The pain is most commonly felt on the outside of the knee but can be felt anywhere along the IT band. I believe this to be a "wobble injury." When the running muscles get tired, they don't keep you on a straight running track. The IT band tries to restrain the wobbling motion, but it cannot and gets overused. Most of the feedback I receive from runners and doctors is that once the healing has started (usually a few days off from running), most runners will heal as fast when you run on it as from a complete layoff. It is crucial to stay below the threshold of further irritation. Stay in touch with your doctor.

TREATMENT FOR IT BAND SYNDROME:

1. **Self-massage using a foam roller**—This device has helped thousands of runners get over IT band pain. See my website *www.jeffgalloway.com* for instruction on using a foam roller. Put the roller on the floor. Lie on it using body weight to press and roll the area that is sore. It helps to warm up the area before a run and to roll it out afterward. Especially helpful is to roll it five minutes before bed.

2. **Massage therapy**—A good massage therapist can tell whether massage will help and where to massage. The two areas for possible attention are the connecting points of the connective tissue that is tight and the fascia band itself in several places. The stick is a self-massage roller device that has also helped many runners recover from IT band pain as they run. As with the foam roller, it helps to warm up the area before a run and to roll it out afterward.

3. **Walking** is usually fine, and usually you can find a run-walk ratio that works.

4. **Direct ice massage on the area of pain**—Do 15 minutes of continuous rubbing every night.

5. **Stretching**—Stretch during a run if the IT band tightens up. There are several stretches that have worked for this injury.

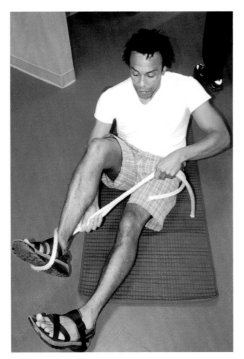

SHIN PAIN—SHIN SPLINTS OR STRESS FRACTURE

Almost always, pain in this area indicates a minor irritation called *shin splints* that allows running and walking as you heal. The greatest pain or irritation during injury is usually felt during the start of a run or walk, which gradually lessens or goes away as you run and walk. It takes a while to fully heal, so you must have patience as you stay below the threshold of further irritation.

» **Inside pain**—Irritation of the inside of the leg coming up from the ankle is called *posterior tibial shin splints* and is often due to over pronation of the foot (foot rolls in at push-off).

» **Front of shin**—When the pain is in the muscle on the front of the lower leg it is *anterior tibial shin splints.* This is very often due to having too long a stride when running and especially when walking. Downhill terrain should be avoided as much as possible during the healing.

» **Stress fracture**—If the pain is in a very specific place and increases as you run, it could be a more serious problem: a *stress fracture.* This is unusual for beginning runners, but characteristic of those who do too much too soon. It can also indicate low bone density. If you even suspect a stress fracture, do not run or do anything stressful on the leg and see a doctor. Stress fractures take weeks of no running, usually wearing a cast. They may also indicate a calcium deficiency.

HEEL PAIN—PLANTAR FASCIA

The most effective treatment is putting your foot in a supportive shoe before your first step in the morning.

This very common injury (pain on the inside or center of the heel) is felt when you first walk on the foot in the morning. As you get warmed up, it gradually goes away, only to return the next morning. The most important treatment is to put your foot in a supportive shoe before you step out of bed. Be sure to get a shoe check at a technical running store to make sure that you have the right shoe for your foot. This is another injury that allows for running as you heal, but stay in touch with your doctor.

If the pain is felt during the day and is noticeable, you should consult with a podiatrist. Usually the doctor will construct a foot support that will surround your arch and heel. This does not always need to be a hard orthotic and is usually a softer one designed for your foot with build-ups in the right places.

The toe squincher exercise can help develop foot strength that will give support to the foot. It takes several weeks for this to take effect. The squincher is done by pointing your foot down and contracting the muscles in the foot similar to making a hard fist with your hand.

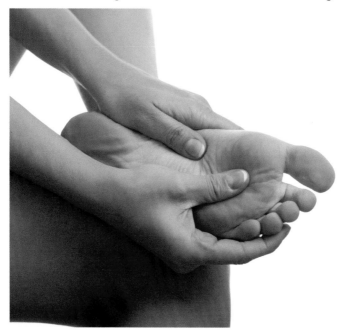

BACK OF THE FOOT PAIN—ACHILLES TENDON

The Achilles tendon is the narrow band of tendon rising up from the heel and connecting to the calf muscle. It is part of a very efficient mechanical system, acting like a strong rubber band to leverage a lot of work out of the foot with a little effort from the calf muscle. It is usually injured due to excessive stretching, either through running or through stretching exercises. First, avoid any activity that stretches the tendon in any way. It helps to add a small heel lift to all shoes, which reduces the range of motion. Every night, rub a chunk of ice directly on the tendon. Keep rubbing for about 15 minutes until the tendon gets numb. Bags of ice or frozen gels don't do any good at all in my opinion. Usually after three to five days off from running, the icing takes hold and gets the injury in a healing mode. Anti-inflammatory medication very rarely helps with the Achilles tendon, according to experts.

HIP AND GROIN PAIN

There are a variety of elements that could be aggravated in the hip area. Since the hips are not prime movers in running, they are usually abused when you continue to push on when very fatigued. The hips try to do the work of the leg muscles but are not designed for this. Ask your doctor about prescription strength anti-inflammatory medication, as this can often speed up recovery. Avoid stretching and any activity that aggravates the area.

CALF MUSCLE PAIN

The calf is the most important muscle for running. It is often irritated by speedwork and can be pushed into injury by stretching, running too fast when tired, too many speed sessions without adequate rest between, and sprinting at the end of races or workouts. Bouncing too high and running a lot of hills can also trigger this injury.

Deep-tissue massage has been the best treatment for most calf muscle problems. Try to find a very experienced massage therapist who has helped lots of runners with calf problems. This can be painful but is about the only way to remove some bio-damage in the muscle. The stick can be very beneficial for working damage out of the calf muscle on a daily basis (see my website, www.JeffGalloway.com, for more information on this product).

Don't stretch! Stretching will tear the muscle fibers that are trying to heal. Avoid running hills and take very frequent walk breaks as you return to running.

26 THE CLOTHING THERMOMETER

A major source of anxiety and needless negative triggers to the reflex brain are weather and clothing concerns. There is no positive effect from worrying about the weather. It will be what it is during the workout or race. You will gain major control over your comfort by using the table below as you prepare for any possibility on race day.

Gaining control over your clothing comfort means having available the various garments listed next for any combination of weather conditions during a workout or race. When packing your bag, look at every weather condition you might encounter on that day and pack your bag accordingly. At race expos, there are usually vendors of major brands, like Mizuno, in case you left something behind. The night before, lay out various combinations of garments that would be appropriate for various weather conditions.

Get up earlier than usual on long run or race mornings and check the weather forecast. The first layer, since it will be next to your skin, should feel comfortable and be designed to wick the moisture away from your skin. You may have to resist the temptation to buy a fashion color, but function is most important. As you try on the clothing in the store, watch for seams and extra material in areas where you will have body parts rubbing together during a run.

Cotton is usually not a good fabric—especially for those who perspire a great deal. The cotton will absorb the sweat, hold it next to your skin, and increase the weight you must carry during the run. This has also been a cause of chaffing. Garments made out of fabric labeled Breath Thermo, Polypro, Coolmax, and Drifit can retain enough body heat to keep you warm in winter while also releasing the extra amount. By moving moisture to the outside of the garment, you will stay cooler in summer and avoid the wind chill in winter. A new fabric by Mizuno, called Breath thermo, actually heats up with modest perspiration in the winter.

Temperature	What to wear
60 °F (14 °C) and above	Tank top or singlet and shorts
50 to 59 °F (9 to 13 °C)	T-shirt and shorts
40 to 49 °F (5 to 8 °C)	Lightweight long-sleeve shirt, shorts or tights (or nylon long pants), mittens and gloves
30 to 39 °F (0 to 4 °C)	Medium-weight long-sleeve shirt and another T-shirt, tights and shorts, socks or mittens or gloves, and a hat over the ears
20 to 29 °F (-4 to -1 °C)	Medium-weight long-sleeve shirt, another T-shirt, tights and shorts, socks, mittens or gloves, and a hat over the ears
10 to 19 °F (-8 to -3 °C)	Medium-weight long-sleeve shirt, and medium- to heavyweight shirt, tights and shorts, nylon wind suit, top and pants, socks, thick mittens, and a hat over the ears
0 to 9 °F (-12 to -7 °C)	Two medium- or heavyweight long-sleeve tops, thick tights, thick underwear (especially for men), medium to heavy warm-up suit, gloves and thick mittens, ski mask, a hat over the ears, and Vaseline covering any exposed skin
-15 °F (-18 to -11 °C)	Two heavyweight long-sleeve tops, tights and thick tights, thick underwear (and supporter for men), thick warm-up suit (top and pants), mittens over gloves, thick ski mask, a hat over ears, Vasoline covering any exposed skin, thicker socks on your feet, and other foot protection, as needed
-20 °F (-20 °C)	Add layers as needed

WHAT NOT TO WEAR

» **A heavy coat in winter**—If the layer is too thick, you'll heat up, sweat excessively, and cool too much when you take it off.

» **No shirt for men in summer**—Fabric that holds some of the moisture will give you more of a cooling effect as you run and walk.

» **Too much sunscreen**—It can interfere with sweating.

» **Socks that are too thick in summer**—Your feet swell, and the pressure from the socks can increase the chance of a black toenail and blisters.

» **Lime green shirt with bright pink polka dots**—Unless you have a lot of confidence and can run fast.

SPECIAL CASES

Chaffing can be reduced by Lycra and other fabric. Many runners have eliminated chaffing between the legs by using a Lycra *bike tight* as an undergarment. These are also called *Lycra shorts*. There are also several skin lubricants on the market, including Glide.

Some men suffer from irritation of their nipples. Having a slick and smooth fabric across the chest will reduce this. There is now a product called NipGuard that has reduced the chance of having this problem.

27 GLOSSARY OF MIND–BODY ELEMENTS

There are a number of body systems, networks, and substances that are constantly monitoring external and internal stress and capabilities, keeping all of the systems working. How they interact will determine which substances are secreted into the receptor molecules, affecting your current emotions and your current level of motivation. The following components are described in a conceptual format so that you can glimpse into the workings of this marvelous system.

Brain—Located in your head, this complex is composed of many components that are constantly processing information. Some are connected in circuits that can work together, and some work separately. There are logical networks and creative ones. The frontal lobe allows humans the ability to take control after monitoring patterns and deciding to change behaviors to get something done.

Conditioning for reflex actions—The control part of the frontal lobe can program the subconscious brain to conduct habitual activities.

Frontal lobe (conscious brain)—This "newer" part of the brain allows humans to understand, plan, and enjoy what they are doing; develop a strategy; make decisions; and search for and understand complex thoughts, experiences, and emotions.

Growth mode—Under normal conditions, when under normal stress for the individual, the reflex brain keeps all functions going, rebuilds damaged areas, replaces worn cells, produces needed energy, and removes waste. Peptides that are produced tell the body and mind that you feel fine and things are good.

Left brain—Located in the frontal cortex, this circuit connects components of logic, judgment, language, math, and other areas. The conscious part of the left brain can take control over our reflex brain.

Ligands—Substances (e.g., hormones, drugs) secreted by the body that bind to the molecule receptors and send and receive information about emotions, beliefs, and behaviors that can change our attitude.

Mind—An interconnected information system throughout the body with communication transmission going on constantly as information hormones (peptides) lock into receptors on billions of cells. The subconscious reflex brain monitors this flow of information and has programmed responses for specific stimuli. The frontal lobe and the right brain can be separately activated when conscious control is needed. When emotions are balanced and positive, the preprogramming has been somewhat consistent and realistic and the system runs smoothly—almost automatically.

Peptides—Ligands that connect the communication system. In the words of Candice Pert, PhD, "Peptides serve to weave the body's organs and systems into a single web that reacts to both internal and external environmental changes with complex, subtly orchestrated responses."[10]

Protection mode—When stress increases to a high level, the reflex brain protects itself and the organism by increasing blood flow to the limbs and to the reflex brain. At the same time, blood flow is constricted to the frontal lobe, digestive, immune, and waste removal

---

10   Pert, C. 1997. *Molecules of Emotion.* New York: Scribner, 148.

systems. For a short period, the muscles can work at a higher level of activity. This allowed our ancestors to survive threats and can keep us running at a high level of performance until the resources run out. Then, there is an extended recovery time needed. Triggered also by the protection stress are hormones, such as cortisol, which aid in recovery and healing but are also linked to depression and low motivation.

Receptors—Specialized molecules on the surface of a cell where ligands (hormones, drugs, and other substances) can bind so that information can be sent and received—very quickly—throughout body and mind.

Reflex brain (subconscious)—A more primitive area where stimulus–response actions are programmed. Ancient patterns are embedded, which ensured survival long ago, along with programming from childhood. When we learn a new activity by doing it over and over again, we can program this reflex brain to perform automatic patterns of behavior. Here is how Bruce Lipton, PhD describes this entity: "In Reality, the subconscious is an emotionless database of stored programs whose function is strictly concerned with reading environmental signals and engaging in hardwired behavioral programs, no questions asked, no judgements made."[11]

Right brain—This non-verbal, unconscious circuit connects areas of creativity and intuition. Mental training techniques can empower the right brain to find creative solutions, tap hidden resources, and allow you to do what you are capable of doing—even if you don't know that you are capable of doing so.

---

11   Lipton, B. 2005. *Biology of Belief.* Carlsbad: Hay House, Inc., 135.

28 PRODUCTS THAT ENHANCE RUNNING

JEFF GALLOWAY TRAINING APPS BY LOLOFIT

It's my voice coaching you through the workouts to prepare for and then race a 5K, 10K, half marathon, or marathon. You can use your music or that provided on the app. Special effect is that as the pace picks up, so does the beat of the music.

THE BFF

This vibrating massage tool is second only to a really good massage therapist in reviving sore or tired muscles. The vibration motion increases blood flow, stimulates the muscle cells, and feels good.

THE STICK

This massage tool can help the muscles recover quicker. It will often speed up the recovery of muscle injuries or iliotibial band injuries (on the outside of the upper leg, between knee and hip). This type of device can help warm up the legs muscles and sore tendons before running and move some of the waste out afterward.

When working on the calf muscle (most important in running), start each stroke at the Achilles tendon and roll up the leg toward the knee. Gently roll back to the origin and continue, repeatedly. For the first five minutes your gentle rolling will bring additional blood flow to the area. As you gradually increase the pressure on the calf you will usually find some "knots" or sore places in the muscles. Concentrate on these as you roll over them again and again, breaking up the tightness. See *www.jeffgalloway.com* for more info on this.

FOAM ROLLER — SELF-MASSAGE

The most popular size of this cylinder is approximately 6 inches in diameter and 1 foot long. This has been the most successful treatment device for IT band injury. In treating this injury, put the roller on the floor and lie on your side so that the irritated IT band area is on top of the roller. As your body weight presses down on the roller, roll up and down on the area of the leg you want to treat. Roll gently for two to three minutes and then let the body weight press down more.

This is a very effective pre-warm-up exercise for any area that needs more blood flow as you start. It is also very beneficial to use the roller after a run on the same areas. See *www.jeffgalloway.com* for more info on this product.

ACCELERADE

This sports drink has a patented formula shown to improve recovery. It also helps to improve hydration. I recommend having some in the refrigerator as your fluid intake product taken throughout the day. Prime time to drink this regularly is the day before and after a long or strenuous workout day. During a prolonged speed training session, have a thermos nearby for sipping on walk breaks.

Research has also shown that drinking Accelerade about 30 minutes before running can get the body's start-up fuel (glycogen) activated more effectively and may conserve the limited supply of this crucial fuel. For a discount on this product, go to *www.JeffGalloway.com* and click on the "Accelerade" logo.

ENDUROX R4

This product has what I see as a cult following among runners. In fact, the research shows that the 4:1 ratio of carbohydrate to protein helps to reload the muscle glycogen more quickly. This means that the muscles feel bouncy and ready to do what you can do sooner. There are other antioxidants that speed recovery. Prime time for this reloading process is within 30 minutes of finishing a run. For a discount on this product, go to www. JeffGalloway.com and click on the "Accelerade" logo.

27.1 OTHER GALLOWAY BOOKS, TRAINING SCHEDULES, AND GIFTS THAT KEEP ON GIVING—EVEN TO YOURSELF

(Order autographed copies from www.JeffGalloway.com.)

THE RUN WALK RUN METHOD

Jeff's innovative ideas have opened up the possibility of running and completing a marathon to almost everyone. Philosophically, Jeff believes that we were all designed to run and walk, and he keeps finding ways to bring more people into the positive world of exercise.

NUTRITION FOR RUNNERS

Using material from renowned nutritionist Nancy Clark, Jeff Galloway gives the reader tips on what to eat, when to eat, how much to eat, and how to combine all that with your training schedule while still retaining the chance to enjoy other aspects of life.

TRAIL RUNNING

Jeff Galloway teaches you to start trail running the right way with his unique way of guaranteeing an injury free running style. The book covers training plans for beginners and advanced runners as well as a wide range of trail running equipment, especially the whole range of trail running shoes.

AMERICA'S BEST PLACES TO RUN

This book enhances the running experience by offering access to very special running routes. It gives a preview of the scenery with directions to the start and special instructions to enjoy the area. The book also includes tips on training for trail running, dealing with elevation, running uphill and downhill, terrain issues, and endurance.

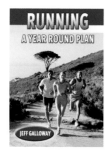

RUNNING: A YEAR ROUND PLAN

This is my most comprehensive training book. It has all of the elements scheduled, leading to goal races of 5K, 10K, half marathon, and marathon. It weaves the training for several races at one time. You'll find daily workouts for 52 weeks for three levels of runners: to finish, to maximize potential, and to improve time. It has the long runs, speed sessions, drills, and hill sessions all listed in the order needed to do a 5K, 10K, half, and marathon during one year. Resource material is included to help with many running issues.

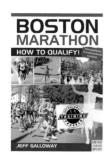

BOSTON MARATHON: HOW TO QUALIFY

Training is listed for each of the qualifying times for Boston. You'll find a listing of the courses that have produced the highest percentage of Boston qualifying finishers. My friend Bill Rodgers (four-time Boston champion) helped me provide a guide on how to run the Boston course. There are several enhanced training tips to maximize performance that are not included in other books, along with nutrition, motivation, and lots of other information.

CROSS-COUNTRY RUNNING

This is a complete guide for training and racing off road for 5K, 2 mile, and 1 mile. There are sections on team strategies, mental training, nutrition, recovery, and much more.

GALLOWAY'S MARATHON FAQ: OVER 100 OF THE MOST FREQUENTLY ASKED QUESTIONS

There are over 100 of the most common questions I receive about marathon training and racing. You don't have to wade through pages of text to get the answers to your questions.

RUNNING UNTIL YOU'RE 100, THIRD EDITION

In the chapter on joint health, you'll see in the research studies that runners have healthier joints than sedentary people. In the chapter on the researched health benefits of exercise, an expert on longevity says that for every hour we exercise, we can expect to get back two hours of life extension. Among the heroes section is an 85-year-old who recently finished his 700th marathon and will do 29 more in one year. There are nutrition suggestions from Nancy Clark, training adjustments by decade, and many other helpful hints for running past the century mark.

FIT KIDS – SMARTER KIDS

This book is a handbook for parents, teachers, and youth leaders on how to lead kids into fitness that is fun. A growing number of studies are listed that document how kids who exercise do better in academics and in life. Nancy Clark gives tips on what to eat, and there's a chapter on childhood obesity with the hope that others, like the author (a former fat kid), can turn things around. There are resources, successful programs, inspirational stories, and much more.

WOMEN'S COMPLETE GUIDE TO RUNNING

The section on woman-specific issues makes this book unique: pregnancy, menstrual issues, bra-fitting, incontinence, osteoporosis, inner organs shifting, menopause and more. There's a section for the unique problems of the "fabulously full figured" runners. Nutrition, fat-burning, motivation, starting up, aches and pains—all are covered in the book. There's also a section in the book written by famous sports nutritionist Nancy Clark.

RUNNING AND FAT BURNING FOR WOMEN

I've not seen another book that better describes the fat burning and accumulation process with a strategy to take action. There are several important and inexpensive tools mentioned, with recipes, and specific suggestions about managing the calorie income and expenditure. There is also a section on women-specific issues.

WALKING: A COMPLETE BOOK

Walkers now have a book that explains the many benefits of walking and how to maximize them, with training programs for 5K, 10K, and half and full marathons. There is resource information on fat burning, nutrition, motivation, and much more.

RUNNING: GETTING STARTED

This is more than a state-of-the-art book for beginners. It gently takes walkers into running with a six-month schedule that has been very successful. Also included is information on fat burning, nutrition, motivation, and body management. This is a great gift for your friends or relatives who can be "infected" positively by running.

RUNNING INJURIES: TREATMENT AND PREVENTION

Dave Hannaford is one of the best resources I've found in explaining why we get injured and how to heal. He breaks down each major running injury to help you diagnose, treat, and heal. I have written the section on prevention, based upon more than 30 years of no overuse injuries.

GALLOWAY'S BOOK ON RUNNING, SECOND EDITION

This is the bestseller among running books since 1984. Thoroughly revised and expanded in 2001, you'll find training programs for 5K, 10K, half marathon, and marathon, with nutrition, fat burning, walk breaks, motivation, injuries, shoes, and much more. This is a total resource book

MARATHON: YOU CAN DO IT

This has the latest marathon training and racing information. It was revised in 2010.

GALLOWAY TRAINING PROGRAMS

This has the information you need to train for the classic event, the marathon. It also has schedules for the half marathon and 10 mile. This has the latest on walk breaks, long runs, practical nutrition, the magic mile, mental marathon toughness, and much more.

HALF-MARATHON: YOU CAN DO IT

This new book provides highly successful and detailed training schedules for various time goals for the half marathon. Information is provided on nutrition, mental preparation, fluids, race-day logistics and checklist, and much more.

5K/10K RUNNING

Whether you want to finish with a smile on your face or have a challenging time goal in mind, this book is a total resource for these distances. There are schedules for a wide range of performances; information on how to eat, how to predict your performance, how long, and how fast to run on long runs; and drills to improve form and speed training. There is extensive information on mental preparation, breaking through barriers, practical nutrition, and more.

JEFF GALLOWAY'S TRAINING JOURNAL

Some type of journal is recommended to organize and track your training plan. *Jeff Galloway's Training Journal* can be ordered, autographed, from *www.JeffGalloway.com*. It simplifies the process with places to fill in information for each day. There is also space for recording the unexpected thoughts and experiences that make so many runs come alive again as we read about them.

RUNNING SCHOOLS AND RETREATS

I conduct motivating running schools and retreats. These feature individualized information, form evaluation, comprehensively covering running, nutrition, and fat burning.

27.2 VITAMINS

I now believe that most runners need a good vitamin to help the immune system and resist infection. There is some evidence that getting the proper vitamin mix can speed recovery. The vitamin line I use is called Cooper Complete. Dr. Kenneth Cooper is behind this product. In the process of producing the best body of research on exercise and long-term health I've seen anywhere, he found that certain vitamins help in many ways.

BUFFERED SALT TABLETS

These reduce cramping. If your muscles cramp on long or hard runs, this type of product may help greatly. The buffered sodium and potassium tablets get into the system more quickly. Be sure to ask your doctor if this product is OK for you (those with high blood pressure, especially). If you are taking a statin drug for cholesterol and are cramping, it is doubtful that this will help. Ask your doctor about adjusting the medication before long runs.

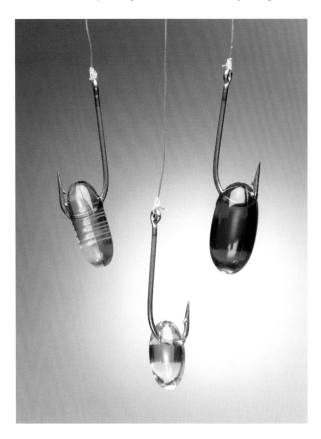

EPILOGUE:
CREDIT WHERE CREDIT IS DUE

I was fortunate to have been taught by some great teachers and thinkers at Westminster Schools in Atlanta and Wesleyan University in Connecticut. In many classes I debated the issue of whether genetics or environment was the primary influence on human behavior and evolution. While I have always acknowledged the opportunity of an individual to make choices, the paradigm of my educational experience (1960s) predicted that genetics and DNA were the primary determinant in behavior. Human evolution, according to many thinkers in the 60s, was creating a rift between mind and body. Genetically, brains could do amazing things, producing a separation from the primitive instincts of the body. The trend seemed to be clear: If we had the right genetics, our mind would be capable of navigating us through life, while the frailties of the body could divert us from our potential. So the concept was that of a hierarchical structure of the brain dictating what the body should do. Then came volumes of research showing that this was not the case.

My experience in my career has shown me that those who seemingly had no physical ability and led sedentary and unfulfilled lives for years have turned their lives around by setting an endurance goal using running and walking. For more than 35 years, I've heard thousands of success stories, and I've come to believe that most of us can gain control over our attitude and can find inside ourselves the motivation we need to stay on track, to overcome challenges, and to break through barriers.

During the past 10 years, my wife Barbara has introduced me to the work of others who have come to similar conclusions and explained the biological reasons behind these changes. In several sections of this book I have referred to the work of John Ratey, MD, Bruce Lipton, PhD, Candace Pert, PhD, and John Sarno, MD. Each has made major contributions in scientifically documenting how the mind and body are embedded and how individuals can change behavior patterns. Since we are, to a great extent, what we do and what we think about, the choices we make each day determine who we are and what we will become.

Dr. John Ratey, in his book *Spark*, details how exercise improves brain function–immediately and long term.

Dr. Brue Lipton is a cellular biologist who has conducted landmark research on how genes are controlled by an individual's perception of the environment. When mind, body, and spirit are focused on change, a process of evolution can bring it about.

Dr. Candace Pert conducted breakthrough research while at National Institutes of Health, Georgetown University Medical Center, and other institutions. She discovered the cellular receptors for endorphins and explained the information network of hormones throughout the body responds to our beliefs and thoughts.

Dr. John Sarno has spent a career helping people overcome orthopedic problems through understanding tension myositis syndrome (TMS). His vast clinical experience with a very high cure rate has shown that a significant percentage of individuals with chronic pain are suffering from the effects of stress, which triggers an unconscious reduction of blood flow to damaged areas.

I endorse the following books and highly recommend them:

Biology of Belief by Bruce Lipton (Hay House, Inc, 2005)

Molecules of Emotions by Candace B. Pert (Scribner, 1997)

The Mindbody Connection by John E. Sarno (Wellness Central, 1998)

Spark by John Ratey (Little, Brown and Company, 2007)

CREDITS

Copyediting:	Elizabeth Evans
Cover design:	Andreas Reuel
Cover photo:	© Thinkstockphotos/moodboard
Design and typesetting:	Andreas Reuel
Photos:	© Thinkstockphotos/Stockbyte: Page 9, 22, 148, 182
	© Thinkstockphotos/Hemera: Page 16, 96
	© Thinkstockphotos/iStock: Page 20, 40, 138, 196, 205
	© Thinkstockphotos/alphaspirit: Page 26
	© Thinkstockphotos/lzf: Page 36, 46, 114
	© Thinkstockphotos/Thomas Northcut: Page 52
	© Thinkstockphotos/Digital Vision: Page 60, 203
	© Thinkstockphotos/Jupiterimages: Page 66
	© Thinkstockphotos/Maridav: Page 86
	© Thinkstockphotos/Jacob Ammentorp Lund: Page 104
	© Thinkstockphotos/mel-nik: Page 108
	© Thinkstockphotos/PHOTOS.com: Page 124
	© Thinkstockphotos/Ammentorp Photography: Page 130
	© Thinkstockphotos/BrianAJackson: Page 152
	© Thinkstockphotos/Oleksandr Briagin: Page 156